EMPOWER
The Now

ANTOINETTE SPURRIER

Empower The Now

Copyright © 2014 by Antoinette Spurrier

All rights reserved. No part of this book may be reproduced or transmitted in any form or by any means without written permission of the author.

ISBN: 978-0-9903824-3-0 (paperback)

*You are invited to claim true
personal and spiritual empowerment
by deepening your awareness of
your connection with Spirit.*

Contents

Introduction 1

I   Creating Deliberate Happiness 3

II Our Dual Nature:
    The Limited Self and the Eternal Self 41

III Empower The Now 69

IV Epilogue 127

Acknowledgments

Collaborators

Andrew Freedman,
wordsmith who was the keeper of the intention; he expanded the book in scope, vitality and heart.

Jacqui Freedman,
artistic contributor who captures Spirit and Nature in her light-filled watercolors. Her work is available through Jacquifree@yahoo.com

Sherry (Heidi) Hall,
the woman with the velvet voice and empathetic heart, who gave inspirational input.

Deborah Probst Kayes,
proofreader, coordinator, sustainer, and multi-tasker with extraordinary tenacity and patience.

Becky Lawton,
provider of multifaceted contributions.

Suresh Ramaswamy,
creative webmaster for FieldsOfLight.com

Anne Marie Welsh,
editor and dynamic catalyst for the birthing process of *Creating Deliberate Happiness: The Complete Guide* and this series.

Mark Murphy,
aka Mr. Creativity who provided graphic art input and inspiration.

Special Mention

The Foundation for Personal and Spiritual Empowerment
FieldsOfLight.com

The San Diego Foundation

My gratitude and appreciation also go to: Martin Anthony, Dr. James Ajemian, Rebecca and Todd Astill, Dr. Concepcion Barrio, The Bectold Family, Lou Bewersdorf, Wendell and Elaine Blonigan, Sheila Byrne, Renee and Sophia Carson, Kea Christina, Cathi Eggleston, Joseph Escoffier, Susann and Richard Fishman, Paul Gorsuch, Norma Grey, Kari Kashani, Nikki Mann, Sandra and Geoffrey Mavis, Deirdre Maher, Alveda and Weston Maughan, John McLaurin, Patrick and Catherine McNabb, Anne McQuillan, Kevin McQuillen, Ron and Marlane Miriello, Dr. Carl and Chris Murphy, Chaitanya Narayan, Jim and Kathleen Newcomb, Brian and Emily Quinn, Francisco Reynoso, Brian and Alison Ross, Jan Saucier, Jeffrey Spurrier, David and Rose Spurrier, Ann Summa, Lisa Baker Scurr & Ron Scurr, Ricardo Torres-Roldan and Family, Penny Wing.

In Memoriam

John Laurence,
teacher, mentor and spiritual advisor. He was blessed with spiritual gifts that he shared unselfishly with others. He was instrumental in who I have become.

John McLaurin,
who personified friendship and sustained constancy, loyalty and love in that friendship. We journeyed together in the past and will do so again.

Linda Provence Diehl,
a beloved friend who expressed in wonderful ways both analytical thought and intuitive knowing. She made everyone feel that she had the ability to be mother to all.

Charles Mirandon,
who contributed through his friendship and loving support of our family and projects for more than 40 years.

Introduction

To the Reader,

My desire is to inspire you to remember that you are essentially a spiritual being and as such, possess a vast inner power radiant in its potential to create, inspire, and lead you to deliberate happiness. Achieving this sense of empowerment means making yourself a creative actor in your own life. When you live an empowered life, you live a more loving life—in the Here and Now in connection with Spirit. Yet so many themes, issues and emotions interfere with the ability to feel empowered, to pursue happiness and to know who you truly are.

You may identify so powerfully with the body and mind as you perceive them or attach so powerfully to ideas about what happiness will look like, that you may feel you are grasping mist as you live mentally in the past and the future instead of the Now. Your habits in consciousness are another major deterrent to experiencing peace, happiness and joy. But you can frame and reframe experiences and employ journaling and meditation as steps on the path toward true empowerment, both personal and spiritual. You may have to explore your ideas about whether there is just one self, defined by its identification with the body and its material realm, an identification that may block your discovery of the real self. You may need to ask "Who is it *really* that journeys in this life."

And so, I invite you to reflection and action by providing spiritual principles and techniques, including affirmations, that can help you turn any feelings of impotence or confusion into a sense of your great innate power as a spiritual creature, a child of the Divine.

The topics covered include an analysis of the real meaning of deliberate happiness and a discussion of your two selves, the Limited and the Eternal, as well as practical tools for integrating the two.

My intention is to assist you in claiming your essential spiritual connection and knowledge. Achieving that, you will always stand firm in your personal and spiritual empowerment. And as you better understand spiritual principles and these techniques, you will attract more love into your life, eventually returning to your natural state of happiness, on the path to joy.

Congratulations on taking the first step!

Antoinette Spurrier

CHAPTER I

Creating Deliberate Happiness

You have the innate capacity to be happy and experience joy now. That ability is rooted in the truest part of your own nature, the essence of who you are!

KEY CONCEPTS:
- Happiness: not what you find, but what you create.
- Self-exploration and journaling.
- Preconceptions about happiness.
- Ideas that limit your access to more happiness.
- The spiritual essence of your true nature.
- Self-knowledge and self-assessment.
- Your hidden happiness contract.
- Steps in creating greater happiness.
- Changing consciousness to change circumstances.
- The two parts of your consciousness.

The Power of the Universe is Within You

You can become a dynamic creator of your own deliberate happiness because you contain within yourself part of the power of all creation. That power may be hiding from your skittering mind and restless consciousness, yet your hidden treasure, nevertheless, remains to be discovered. This book offers practices and helpful tools to aid in your treasure-hunting quest. But the irony is that *you* are the treasure you seek. The map you use will take you home to your own empowered consciousness, for you cannot address the subject of happiness without also emphasizing your own quest for personal empowerment.

You may wonder why the map to your happiness has been so obscure, and the path so strewn with obstacles thwarting your progress. One of the greatest of these roadblocks may be your habits in consciousness. To become more empowered necessitates becoming more aware of these thought patterns. Then you may resolve to change by using techniques that include introspection and self-analysis, breaking the worry habit, being present in the Now, cultivating peace and a consciousness of even-mindedness, and by spiritual practices such as meditation, visualization and affirmations.

Do consider the ways in which your own habitual thinking contaminates your happiness, your wellspring of joy, but please, don't go into overwhelm mode! Rather, observe your present habits in consciousness as a smoke screen that may prevent you from seeing and being aware of your inner essence and power. Fortunately that power is still alive and well, dynamic and exciting within you. Your treasure hunt is the quest to awaken to that truth. The many helpful techniques mentioned above are not the goal: To become awake and empowered in your consciousness and your life is the destination of a journey that you take one step at a time. Resolving to try is the first step. Take that first step onto the path.

The treasure map is unfolding. You *can* find your way home again when you discover the dynamic creator within yourself. A consciousness focused in dynamic creation can be yours. It is yours already.

The Power and the Art of Creating Happiness
It's not what you find, but what you create

I can see it now. The looming metal presence dwarfed the ones I had seen before. Ahead of me was not only the ultimate "fun" experience, but happiness itself! The park's slippery slide—my image of happiness—stood baking in the blazing sun. Our picnic lunch was being unloaded while we kids were running about. Yet for me, the sounds of those picnickers dimmed in the background.

I had always wanted to try out that slide. But usually, it was only the bigger kids who rode the big one. My long-held desire and fantasy were seducing me to the big ride, but adults insisted on lunch first. I knew the unwritten rules of our picnics: excessive eating; people talking exuberantly over one another; some adult setting down rules; my mother, ever the advocate, chiming in, "Oh they're just kids, couldn't they just do one _____ (fill in the blank with wild behavior and great mischief and risky adventures). We were lucky to have an advocate strengthening the kids' choir of "Please can't we _____ etc., etc."

But other voices overlaid our kids' choir. "Hey, kids, stop running in the sprinklers!" Our retort: "Oh, but it's such a hot day, what can it hurt?"

For the moment, though, this was background noise. I was transfixed, actually hypnotized by the big slide. It was staring me down, not with eyes, but with dancing sunlight. Seeing it up close, it appeared even larger than I remembered, and a container of possibilities. Yes, the big slide, fun and happiness itself.

First came the feast, the picnic indulgences. Always sandwiches, mine with a giant chunk of lettuce on top of home grown, sun-ripened tomatoes that dripped mayonnaise on chins and clothes, and below the tomatoes, more layers of meat and cheese. My Aunt Clara, famous for her potato salad, reminded us, "Our family knows how to eat. We never use that puffy nonsense bread. You'll know a family by the bread they eat." We agreed that someday she would be famous for her potato salad not just in our family but throughout the world.

Then watermelon slices miraculously appeared, along with potato salad, fresh fruit, dill pickles, more excessive sandwiches, and Aunt Donna's homemade apple pie with luscious, rich Snelgrove vanilla ice cream for dessert. Normally, I would then lead "let's run through the sprinklers," and listen to adult conversations and savor and remember every morsel of food. But not this day, which offered a muted experience, slipping past even while I went through the motions of living it, because happiness, undiluted happiness, was ahead, calling to me.

My consciousness was engaged in that goal, and so, leaving my food unfinished, I ran for the big slide. Others followed in pursuit, even leaving their pie and ice cream unfinished.

"Com'on, com'on, we're going to do it!" The joy of anticipation spurred us forward. The older boys beat the younger cousins in this race to the slides. Even while sprinting, I had time to ponder the big sparkling slide and the greater possibilities it offered for the descent. Shaking with excitement and fear—after all, the slide was an oversized metal giant—I heard Wayne call out "Careful, you're running on the backs of prisoners."

I looked but didn't see any backs or prisoners. I did know the carefully manicured park was built on the old prison grounds, but this was an offsetting thought before the perfect experience that awaited on the slide. Thoughts of the prisoners disturbed me as I began climbing the tall, hot stairs to the metal giant's top. On such a hot day, the metal railings burned my hands as I climbed, still visibly shaking and anticipating the perfect happiness of my whoosh down the slide.

Up top I began mentally talking to myself with fear-driven excitement. *It's too high here. Why do they let little kids climb so high here? Maybe I could do this later.*

I would have postponed the big event but the boys were pushing from behind, and I didn't want them to know I was scared. Propelled forward by the motion of the upcoming collective body of children, I finally made the complicated effort to sit. Then the full vision of the terrifying, steep drop opened before me.

"Hurry up, hurry up," the children's choir sang again.

Suddenly I realized I could die going down that thing, but I was being spurred onward by the more assertive boys. "Go down or get off!"

And so I went down, though I don't recall the frightening descent. Instead I felt my flesh searing on the metal of the slide because my legs were completely exposed to the summer sun. When I hit the bottom, I ran fast and shaking to the refuge of my picnicking family of adults. I heard their concern.

"Look, something's wrong!"

"She has a burn. She got burned on that metal slide."

"Come here, dear. I'll get some ice."

Trembling, saddened, disappointed, afraid. My day of such possibilities, a day full of fun, a picnic, a park and happiness personified by that slippery slide gleaming in the sunlight delivered instead burns on my hands and legs. My hope and prospective happiness were fried by the sun's rays. I began to wonder how do you find joy running on the backs of prisoners, climbing slides that are too high, made of metal that burns flesh on the rapid descent downward. Happiness had seemed possible, probable, even inevitable.

Instead I vowed never to ride down the slippery slide again, but of course I forgot the vow and even the burns and later took many more downward rides on the slippery slide.

My family soothed my disappointment as they always did, for they believed that true cures involved food. "Come here, I've got some of your favorites here: pie with ice cream and some of Diane's pickles. Then we'll get more ice for the burns."

Even the food that normally brought me such delight failed to dispel the unhappiness that welled up from some place deep inside. My focus had been so exclusively on the slide, I had missed out on everything else, even my family's "bread wisdom: You can know a family by the bread they eat." (Evidently a bread of substance reflected a family of substance.) Neither food nor family wisdom helped my despair.

Intuitively, even then, I knew I would need that knowledge. But that summer day was also providing me with knowledge that I would later internalize and make a central theme of my larger book, *Creating Deliberate Happiness: The Complete Guide*.

Central Themes on Creating Deliberate Happiness

1. The greater our attachment and desire for the object or objects of our desire, the less likely it is that they will produce the desired happiness.
2. The more we personify what happiness will look like, the less we create from an expanded vision of ourselves, others and circumstances. Narrowness of vision constricts possibilities.
3. Living in the past or future creates muted experiences. Living in the Now is our true key to the happiness we seek.

Most of us have experienced the kind of disappointment I did as a child who so desperately wanted to plunge down the big slide. Most of us have realized that we were sometimes chasing after happiness in the wrong places. And most of us have made such vows as I did—never to seek happiness pursuing goals that have eluded or saddened us before. And most of us have broken those vows, or merely changed our vision of the goal or achievement or place that will bring us happiness. That is because most people refer to "finding" happiness, as if it were a commodity located somewhere else. But where is it located?

Perhaps you tie your happiness to achieving recognition from others, or to acquiring material possessions or professional success, equating success with happiness. Yet many who are highly "successful" actually possess deeply troubled lives filled with emotional upheaval and personal unhappiness. Believing that there is a direct relationship between success and happiness will channel your energy into the world to acquire more from the material plane of existence. Like the hot metal slide of my childhood, material things seldom satisfy, and rarely for long.

In reality, your happiness is tied primarily to the state of your consciousness rather than to the conditions around you. You may feel happiness is external to yourself, dependent on your relationships with others and dictated by your circumstances. But those circumstances are not separate from your actions and your consciousness. Your life reflects the habitual patterns in your consciousness. Your life is the moving mirror of your consciousness. You can deliberately create greater happiness by rooting out tenacious habits of negative thought and instead watering positive thoughts with truth and self-love.

New possibilities emerge when you seek the happiness and joy that emanates from the core of your being instead of from the material world. The winds of discontent that appear to blow us about unanchored may be but the whisper of a silent God calling us homeward to our natural state of joy. Have you reflected on these thoughts? You are a dynamic creator capable of owning peace and creating deliberate happiness.

The good news (and the bad news) is that happiness is not a location, nor is it an object to be found. It is not a person to be possessed, or a separate individual who holds the key to your happiness. The happiness map does not solely involve the terrain of the physical, material world. Above all things, it involves a journey in expanded, cultivated awareness achieved through the necessary steps of self-exploration. These techniques create foundational change and fully grounded transformation. In outline form, these techniques include:

- Exploring consciousness.
- Dialoging to know and claim the self.
- Journaling to know the self and access its creativity.
- Uprooting deservedness issues.
- Meditation to achieve peace and inner knowing.
- Affirmations to unlock the potent power of your self.
- Visualization tapping the power of your imagination.

This journey, in the end, will lead to a place of expanded consciousness where you will begin to perceive who you truly are. In that knowing, you become capable of achieving higher states of happiness and wellbeing. Obstacles to self-discovery appear when you do not know or have forgotten that you possess both a physical and a divine nature. We will explore these two selves—Limited and Eternal—extensively in Chapter Three on your dual nature.

Exploring Preconceptions Around Happiness

Let us examine a prevalent societal myth and why that myth is false and destructive to feeling empowered and finding real happiness.

> **Societal Myth:** *The source of my happiness is <u>external</u> to myself and is dependent upon other people, things, conditions or circumstances.*

This myth is false because happiness is tied primarily to a greater awareness of your own consciousness and true nature. Your <u>internal</u> perceptions, interpretations and habits in consciousness are more important than external circumstances. Happiness expands as you deepen your experience of being alive and of your own spiritual nature.

Limiting Ideas Around the Subject of Happiness

Some common ideas that may hamper your being happy are:

- My happiness is tied to the past.
- My happiness is tied to the future.
- My happiness depends upon achieving certain desirable conditions and circumstances.
- My happiness requires possessing a person, object, fulfilled desire, financial success, wealth or prosperity, the love of the right person, the recognition of the right people, success in an exciting career, removal of a current obstacle or threat, etc.
- Happiness will not be mine until I am healthy, prosperous and live in ideal conditions.

Common Misconceptions About Happiness

I will be happy when:

- Someone else truly understands me.
- I find the right person to love.
- I have a committed, lasting relationship.
- I have children.
- My children will be old enough to be on their own.
- Another person apologizes for the harm done to me.
- I make more money.
- I look different than I do now.
- I am more successful.
- I am famous.
- I am rich, powerful, and important.
- I have a new house, car, boat, airplane, jewelry, etc.
- I finish school or I have more degrees.
- I have a new job.
- I am in a different career.
- I have meaningful work.

Journaling – a tool in greater self-discovery

Journaling allows us to know ourselves better, and it also can create a map for our life's journey. Throughout this book you will encounter journaling activities to help clarify your own ideas and open fresh windows of introspection—if you journal honestly, deeply and regularly.

Journaling supports your journey of discovery. Writing your answers to the suggested prompts may give you a deeper self-understanding beyond the superficial mental level of your ideas about yourself.

If you are to create more happiness in your life, you need to explore your personal perspective on the subject. In writing an assessment of your present state of happiness, you are beginning a more substantial dialogue on your life's journey. You also create a baseline to examine your growth and see your capacity for the state of mind necessary to achieve enduring happiness.

Please complete the journal exercises in the spirit of self-discovery. You may be in a state of perfect health, and have abundant opportunities and meaningful relationships, but you may still feel unhappy or dissatisfied. You may see happiness as a goal of the future, unattainable in the present. But danger lurks in thinking "I will be happy later." That becomes an affirmation in which you tell yourself, "Don't be happy now. You can't be happy now. Be happy later." Such ideas poison the Now. The Now is all you have and all you will ever have in life.

> *When we approach journaling with an open mind and heart, and we commit to being completely candid with ourselves, we open up to limitless opportunity for growth and healing. Through total honesty, we begin to peel away the layers of our psyche. The masks we wear begin to fall away, revealing our true nature – who we are when we aren't "the parent, the employee, the friend" and are just ourselves.*
>
> CHRISTIN SYNDER,
> *The Healing Power of Journaling*

Going Deeper:
Are You Happy Now?

Write your answers to these questions about your present state of emotional fulfillment and contentment:

- Is your daily frame of mind peaceful and joy-filled?
- How much is your happiness tied to the past?
- How much is it tied to the future?
- How much is tied to career or to expectations around others?
- Is your idea of happiness tied to a future experience, or desire?
- Is happiness in your life on the installment plan?
- If so, how many years ahead do you expect that contentment, inner satisfaction, and happiness will arrive?
- Does your desire to acquire or possess in any way violate the wellbeing, or the happiness, of another person?

Simply because you desire to acquire or possess something does not give you free license to pursue that object of desire. There does exist a moral imperative not to thwart the happiness or wellbeing of other people by pursuing your own desires. Yet some people may abandon their deep inner dreams because of a fear of hurting or disappointing others.

Clarity about your right to pursue those dreams will come from inner discourse and honoring others, without suspending the right to make decisions you know are proper for yourself. Clarity and integrity in self-dialogue are necessary elements in analyzing yourself, your dreams, and your goal of happiness. Seeming happiness tends not to last if you have suspended your moral compass.

After you have completed your initial list in the journaling exercise, note how many items or desires are tied to the external world. Then count how many of your notations emphasize accessing more of yourself through self-discovery. Note themes about how to contribute more to life, or the world, or to serve others as a route to happiness, then consider these questions:

- Do you feel your happiness is tied to the fulfillment experienced in a deep relationship? Or is your idea of happiness tied more to career fulfillment or greater material acquisitions?
- Do you believe that some specific material goal, or career goal, will deliver some state of deep and lasting happiness for you?
- Do you desire deeply to acquire material goods or a specific item of interest and attachment?
- Are your ideas around happiness based in the future or on the idea of happiness in the Now?
- Does happiness for you mean excitement and/or the thrill of pursuing the "ever-evolving new?"
- Is stimulation of the senses the way you feel deep peace and contentment?
- Do you believe that someone else is in possession of the keys to your happiness?
- Does someone else have the power to give it to you or to deprive you of happiness?
- Do you feel deep discouragement rooted in the realization that everything changes?

Inevitably, through the experience of change, we are faced with the impermanence of the things of this world. Often we seem confronted with the truth that our own nature cannot derive lasting contentment from either the mental journey or the pursuit of pleasure in the physical-material world. Yet it is possible that another direction may lead, in the end, to a more permanent state of happiness and contentment. What would that state look like to you? Is there a place within you that can experience serene knowing, deeper truth, and abiding peace, peace that endures despite changing conditions within ourselves and the world? We can find that place if we think of ourselves as human *beings* instead of as busy human *doings*. But how do we discover that place of serene knowing and experience ourselves in a state of being?

Going Deeper Toward Inner Viewing
Is happiness in your life on the installment plan?

The following questions may help you deepen your understanding of your personal perspective on happiness:

- How did your mother define a successful life?
- How did your father define a successful life?
- How are these ideas the same or different from your own?
- On a scale from 1-10, 10 being the most happy, how would you rate the overall state of happiness that your father experienced in his life?
- How would you evaluate your mother's overall level of happiness?

How Your Family Defined a Meaningful Life.

Now write down any thoughts or ideas about how you personally define success and happiness and their interrelationship. Ask yourself how these definitions affected you in the past and whether they continue to impede your life. What is the measuring rod by which you can claim your worth, your success, or your happiness? Are any of the dreams you have embraced a mirror of your parents' dreams?

Journal more about any and all thoughts that come to you on the idea of success and happiness as related to your mother, father, or significant caregivers in childhood. Have you ever considered that any one of your important caregivers may have been significantly depressed? Is it possible that you are experiencing some level of depression yourself? Have you ever been assessed for situational or clinical depression?

If you feel that you are in a chronic state of unhappiness or inner despair, there are several factors that need to be considered. There may be deep thought patterns and feeling states associated with early life experiences. If this material is not examined in a skilled, supportive environment, or if the material is deeply repressed, these issues and feeling states will continue to resurface. Depression itself may have physiological, biological, emotional, or psychological roots. Many individuals exist in an unrecognized state of clinical depression and feel they are under obligation to get "over it" by themselves. If you feel you need to "fix" it yourself, how long have you tried? What has been your success in that effort? Consider getting the help you need in order to empower your life.

More on the Subject of Depression

The result of _not_ seeking professional help may be a life crippled by clinical depression. The tragic reality is that people with clinical depression often respond to psychological or medical intervention. Feeling states of negativity, aloneness, despair, and despondency have roots; they do not exist without causes. Exploring how to remedy this situation can be an opportunity for a rebirth for the individual. There is life and the possibility of joy for those who are ensnared in the web of despair called depression. Never doubt you can be assisted in claiming life once again. Others are willing to support and help you, if you are willing to take the first step—asking for help.

Do You Have a Happiness Contract with Yourself?

Do you have a happiness contract with yourself that is based on pre-conceived ideas? Is your thought pattern dominated by the idea "I will be happy now"? Or is the thought of present happiness lost in projections into the future? Is your happiness contract on the installment plan of future fulfillment? Do you delay claiming your happiness by believing certain conditions must be met in order for you to be happy? What would happen if you decided you can be happy now?

What is a Happiness Contract?

A happiness contract is your belief that happiness will occur if certain conditions are met, or certain desired circumstances manifest. "I will be happy when (blank) occurs in the future" is a perfect example of this conditional thinking. Let us suppose you do have a hidden, or not-so-hidden, contract with yourself around the subject of happiness. How might you clarify both the conscious and subconscious themes that are your preconditions before you can be fully happy? It is important to honestly analyze your self-dialogue around these subjects of preconceived ideas and happiness. It is also important to analyze your own thought processes regarding happiness and success and their relationship to one another. How frustrating it would be if you achieved your desires and still found yourself feeling unfulfilled and disappointed.

Write down that which comes to mind to complete these sentences:

- "I would be happy if…"
- "I will be happy when…"

Keep repeating these sentences, supplying the answers, and then you will be able to see your own inner expectations. You will also be able to explore your internal dialogue around the subject of happiness. The more you dialogue with yourself, the more powerful will be the mirror reflecting you and your self-knowing.

At times we all think in circles; we mentally set up certain contingencies that must occur in our outer circumstances in order for us to be happy. Explore those expectations and ideas to reveal the potent dialogue you engage in with yourself. These ideas become an increasingly energized force field, deepening your attitudes as you repeat and replay them in your mind. These ideas and expectations possess their own energized reality. This reality is not based on the substance of truth nor clarity of perception, but rather on the repetition and re-energizing of mental grooves. Those repetitive ideas create a reality that exists because of your charged thoughts. Such charged thoughts have the power to continue creating deeper and deeper grooves with every repetition. You can become a more powerful creator of yourself and your happiness if you clearly see how you are dialoging with your own consciousness and co-creating your future.

You Can Be Happy Now!

You have the power to be happy now. You can achieve more happiness, and more peace, without all of your preconceptions being met. Instead, by achieving greater conscious awareness you can find within yourself greater contentment, peace, serenity, happiness and joy. A shift in consciousness can **empower** you to claim your happiness.

Accessing that deep happiness and greater joy does not always require insight, understanding, or psychological exploration alone. Psychological efforts at self-help and introspection can be potent, often dramatic and powerfully liberating. But beyond psychotherapy, a serious commitment to self-growth by learning the techniques of affirmation and visualization, as well as balanced techniques of meditation, will power your self-claiming on this journey of self-discovery.

Ideas and expectations about what constitutes your happiness can become a self-created contract dictating conditions you think you need to be happy. But when you address yourself from a state of lack, you experience yourself as insufficient. Addressing yourself from a perspective of possibility can transform your life into an experience of opportunity. Expectations are not only the foundation of what you experience, they become the experience itself. As you project your anticipation, you formulate your intention. This formulated intention becomes will-charged, energy-charged and moves into the realm of possibility by acts of imagination, stated intention, and energy-fused creation. Creating meaning during the journey in consciousness requires us to welcome self-exploration.

Steps in Creating Greater Happiness

Creating more happiness involves steps that will help you direct intention towards your self, your life, and your goals. Your intention becomes dynamic by focused imagination and directed will power. Dynamic intention then crystallizes into a commitment. Commitment, itself, then can be directed outward into your life circumstances and intensified by Spirit-charged will power. Following through on commitment creates enhanced feelings of self-worth. These steps, when paired with regular spiritual efforts, deepen your self-knowing and understanding of your nature and consciousness.

- The first step is the **decision and intention** of creating more happiness and joy in your life. Your circumstances follow your dynamic intention.
- Your intention becomes a **commitment** to achieve a state of consciousness that is not primarily dependent on the ebb and the flow of life.

- Charged with will-based energy, your commitment leads to greater **self-valuing, self-knowing, and self-loving**.
- Such enhanced valuing of the self can change your focus to being a **contributor to life** and to others, in harmonious intention with all life.
- Your commitment to **regular spiritual practices** of prayer, visualization, spiritual petitioning, meditation and affirmations accelerates your greater self-knowing.
- When resistance arises, as it inevitably will, you **persevere**. Resistance is a part of true growth and spiritual progress. The negativity of others, your self, and the universe around you does not always embrace your growth and progress. **Continue anyway!**

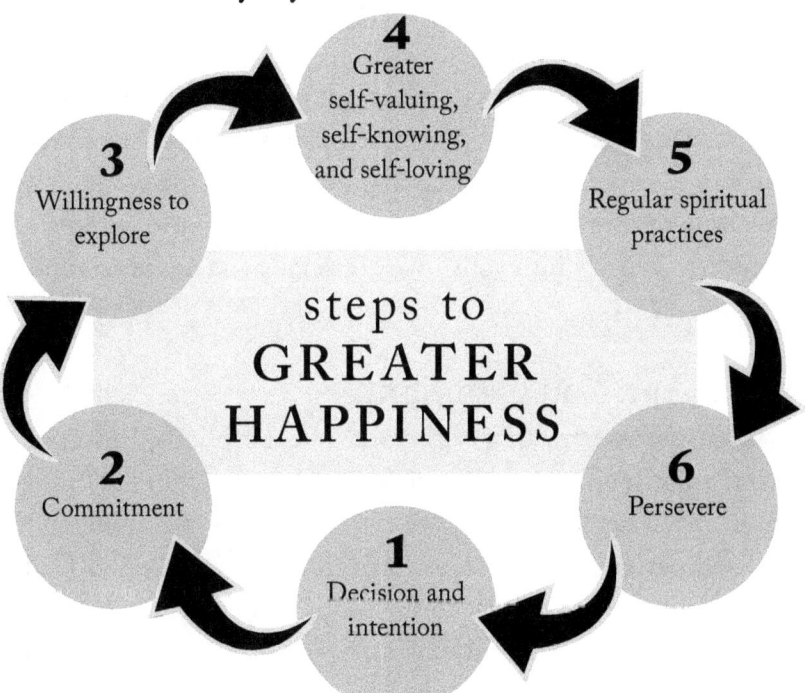

CREATE A DEEPER RELATIONSHIP WITH YOURSELF AND OTHERS!

An essential key to happiness is the development of a deeper relationship with yourself. The more authentic you are with yourself and the more true to your own nature, the greater will be your ability to love yourself and to love others.

In your desire to achieve more happiness, you may naturally be drawn to exploring your inner nature. In that exploration, you will discover not only that Spirit resides within you, but also that you <u>are</u> Spirit. Connecting with your true Self can open you to a new adventure, allowing you to pursue and attain happiness and joy. This quest may also bring powerful change, the unfolding of self-awareness that brings peace and serenity. In this journey of self-discovery you will claim the power that you may have given to others or transferred outside of yourself.

Others lack the capacity to know, understand, and fulfill your deepest needs and desires. Remember, you have no control over the behaviors of others or the external conditions of the world. You *do* have absolute control over your own determination to be on a clear and precise journey into your own consciousness and a relationship with yourself.

WHAT ARE YOU CREATING?

What are you creating with your preconceptions, expectations, interpretations, and attitudes about happiness? Long-standing patterns of thought always impact our capacity for happiness. Our energized patterns in consciousness can become the mind-fields of explosive interference with our pursuit of happiness.

Do you often feel that life happens to you? Do you feel you are in charge of, or have power over, your inner peace, tranquility, or happiness? Do you view yourself as a co-creator of your life? Or have you lost sight of yourself as the author of the drama of your own life? Do you have a sufficient vision of yourself as a creator, a vision that encourages your alignment with the center of your being and the center of all knowing? Do you experience your life as full of discord, or is the vibration of your life experience harmonious and balanced with the universe?

If you will change your circumstances, you must change your consciousness. As your consciousness moves, all circumstances will follow. Changes and movement in your consciousness will create changes in your life. You are a commanding power in the universe.

Take a moment to imagine a new vision of yourself as a potent creator. See yourself aligned with your center of self-knowledge where you can experience the vibration of inner peace. Instead of feeling aligned with a harmonious power in the universe, you may sense life as happening *to* you; if so, you may feel powerless, victimized, and unable to initiate and manifest powerful, lasting change.

Mental activity and energized ideas imprint powerfully on our consciousness. We create with our imagination, our visualization, and energized intention. The more we repeat specific ideas, the more the consciousness is impacted by deep inroads or grooves of mental energy. The more thoughts are repeated along these grooves, the deeper the imprinting in the mental energy field. Repetitive thought patterns gain in power with every repetition.

But you can also create new grooves and unseen possibilities. Believe in your power to create, to manifest, and achieve. An unseen power is in profound connection with you, encouraging your self-knowing, self-exploration, and inner knowledge.

SELF-DISCOVERY IS THE TRUE KEY FOR OUR HAPPINESS

Your ability to access your deeper spiritual nature is the true source of your personal power and peace of mind. This is the premise that enables you to explore your thoughts in order to redefine your life's plan and purpose. As you redefine what you value, you re-prioritize where you place your energy. As you re-prioritize the use of your energy, you claim new energy from the reservoir of Spirit. That energy is yours to access, a sea of love. Its movement can enfold you in inner peace.

You will achieve continuing growth in your ability to access happiness as you realize that true happiness lies within. It is only by deeply knowing the reservoir of Spirit within you that you will achieve growth in personal power. You must cast your pure intention of self-discovery into the energy of the universe with directed will. Your projection of will-based energy and clear intention is the beginning of personal empowerment. By activating and directing the very power of the universe into creation, you will claim more of yourself and the powerhouse of spiritual force.

A deeper connection with your spiritual nature leads to true shifts in consciousness and thus to personal transformation. Your essence, is love-based, joy-based, and light-filled. That higher state of being can bring peace and joy beyond any pursuit of material happiness, for the truth is that the gratification of needs and desires does not bring lasting happiness. Perhaps, like me as a child on that gigantic slide, you have experienced this truth: your needs and desires were fulfilled, yet happiness still eluded you. If so, happiness eluded you because what you believed to be the desired goal did not bring the end of desire. Temporary satiation cannot bring and deepen the joyous vibration of your connection with Spirit. In fact, the more you are identified with your wants, needs, and desires, the less you may wish to contact the core of your being and the vastness of Spirit within.

Awaken Your Inner Knowing; Reframe Your Experiences

To awaken your inner knowing is to discover another, truer part of yourself that often is not experienced but awaits discovery. That discovery can liberate you, for it holds the promise of inner contentment, joy, and self-knowledge.

Nothing has ever occurred to us that did not involve some level of our own participation. Even if you are not the initiator of specific actions, you participate in that which you experience. You may have lacked power over certain events or actions, but no matter what has been taken away from you, if you empower your mind and imagination, you still have the power to interpret events. Your mind, thoughts, and perceptions define and explain your experiences. Mind is the definer and the interpreter, as well as the creator. Your power to interpret, mentally redefine, and reframe your life experiences is a powerful tool of freedom and new creation. When you imagine, you sow the seeds of creation. As you charge energized belief, you deepen the energy of possible creation. Repetition charges these ideas and with energized, will-based mental activity, so that you can create the new.

What if Tragic Circumstances Affect Your Peaceful Self-Knowing?

Even your worst experiences, which you were powerless to prevent, can be reframed in your consciousness by exploring possible avenues of service to others. If you have been in a place of true suffering, nothing will change that experience. But the desire to expand that knowledge of suffering can build a new bridge to others over which your compassion walks. It is a bridge by which others may benefit and a bridge of freedom for you if you feel trapped and powerless over your circumstances. When your feet lack the power to walk to a new way of doing things, trust that the heart has the capacity to grow wings. What you viewed negatively as a traumatic event, you can redefine in mind and imagination as an opportunity. Tragic circumstances may sow the seeds of your creative power, which then blossoms to help yourself and others.

Because you possess consciousness, you possess the power to create, recreate, frame and reframe any and all experiences. No one can take away from you your own imagination. You always possess the power to align with the Source of all creation. Your imagination creates your masterpiece by the act of mental imaging. Together, your consciousness and being form a unified expression of Spirit. You are immutable, unchangeable, and enduring. In the process of awakening this inner knowing, your journey of consciousness may take you into the domain and absolute power of Spirit. You are a diamond light reflection of that Spirit. This discovery awaits you now. Believe you are prepared to make the journey now. You are the discovery itself.

One deterrent to making this discovery and achieving deep happiness may be your self-assessment around the subject of your deservedness. Negative thoughts and feelings may tell you that you do not deserve to be in a place of receiving, discovering and inner-knowing or that you lack the ability to materialize good in your life. These ideas and feelings can merge in powerful mental constructs and energy grooves that inhibit or limit your access to the universal stream of possibilities. When the energy from the Creative Source that created everything and everyone is allowed to flow in your life, you become divinely infused with that energy of all creation. This stream of energy is not separate from the Spiritual

Source; it is the Spiritual Source manifesting itself in you. You are an individualized expression of that Spiritual Source.

Now for the questions:

- How do you align with that Spiritual Source?
- How do you see your own nature – as primarily biological or primarily spiritual?
- Are there ways or means by which you may become more aware of that Source?
- Can you create a greater attunement to that Source itself?
- Is it possible for you to become a better co-producer in the drama of creation and manifestation?
- Do you feel separate and alone, unable to access the Source that created you?
- Do you doubt that there is an Eternal Source from which we all spring?
- Or do you already see yourself as part of that Divine Source on a journey to discover more of your self, your nature, and your true being?

You cannot and should not wait until you feel fully deserving before you act. The universe is a container of both positive and negative forces. You also are a container in which both positive and negative energies are expressed according to actual laws of attraction and repulsion. Negative energy in the universe may tell you that you are not ready to move forward. Those inner statements and feelings of self-doubt may come as whispers of negation. But those whispers contain the negative force of the universe itself, in direct repulsion against the light. They may come as whispers in your ear, but the power and the energy of that negativity resounds into the universe itself.

Sometimes you may doubt that there is a divine light or spiritual energy with love as its essence. If you persevere with intention, you will prove over time the truth of your spiritual existence. You will affirm, with great clarity and internal perception, your connectedness to the light and to all creation. If you go forward, acting as if it is so, even if you do not feel it or believe it yet, you shall begin to see the truth of that testimony of the light.

Spiritually-Based Affirmations:
A Tool to Uproot and Eliminate Deservedness Issues

By systematic repetition of truth contained in Spirit, you may claim your inherent ability to co-create with the Divine. You should not underestimate the power of energized, spiritually-based affirmations in bringing a flow of positive energy into your life. Dynamic intention fused with affirmations creates an energized flow. Will-based affirmations access the power and energy of the force field of creation. Successful people use that principle when they create and experience their own lives. You may also employ that same principle to realize your potential and achieve more success in your inner and outer lives.

Affirmation as used here applies to a specific technique, based on spiritual and scientific principles, that allows for a heightened level of alignment of your consciousness with Spirit. This alignment allows you to tap into the very force of creation and claim more of your true nature. By stating and repeating an affirmation, you claim your nature in words and then these energized words penetrate and expand in deeper recesses of self-knowing. Affirmations used properly have the power to activate more of your spiritual potency. Through the faithful and correct practice and repetition of affirmations, you can align yourself to the truth of your own spiritual nature. An affirmation creates a spiritualized force field expressed in words, with energy, movement and momentum.

Affirmations thus start a potent vibration, which corresponds to both a specific energy frequency and a state of consciousness in seed form. Over time, the affirmation begins to override other smaller vibrations, which eventually become absorbed by the affirmation. Affirmations become power charged by your focused attention and application of will-based energy.

Key General Concepts about Affirmations

Affirmations are an effective technique for change if you desire to:

- Enlarge your sense of personal and spiritual empowerment.
- Change circumstances in your life to a more positive outcome.
- Unleash your creative power by the dynamic force of intention.
- Create new possibilities in your life.
- Explore new talents and new dimensions of yourself.
- Heighten the beneficial use and power of imagination, visualization, and other life-altering techniques.
- Stop negative self-talk and uproot negative tenacious thought patterns that limit your happiness.
- Deepen spiritual life by exploring and expanding consciousness.

Principles Behind Affirmations

- They assist in creating new possibilities in any part of your life.
- They deepen the energy blueprint in creation and stir movement toward manifestation of the desired outcome.
- Creation manifests from energized, repetitive affirmations.

- They increase your ability to develop willpower and discipline.

- Because energy seeks its vibrational counterpart, affirmations seek likeness through magnetic attraction or magnetic repulsion.

- They improve your conditions and circumstances, as you <u>affirm and visualize</u> changed circumstances in a positive, powerful manner. Affirmations thus become charged with your <u>activated will</u>. Creation manifests through this dynamic process, for the power of creation resides in your innate nature.

- The good has the power to continue to create and recreate, operating through the law of magnetic attraction: Like attracts like. As you change your visualizations and utilize affirmations, you exercise your imagination. You change the energy you exude and that which is attracted to you as your energy also shifts. That energy change creates new potency and manifests new creation.

How to Practice Affirmations

Affirmations can be practiced at different times in different states of consciousness:

- Formal waking state.
- Informal waking state.
- Relaxed state.

1. **Decide on your affirmation(s).** Determine, and write down, which affirmation(s) you will be repeating. You may vary from this initial plan, but mentally place your intention on what you desire to affirm. Proceed with sincerity of purpose and certainty that the creative force will become super-charged

by your acts of mental repetition and your regularity and consistency of practice.

2. **Proper posture.** The spine should be erect. You may sit in a straight-back chair, in a relaxed posture, but the spine should be erect and the chin level with the floor. The feet should remain flat on the ground.

3. **Intention of protection** – this both enhances the practice and creates a greater alignment with Spirit.

    a. Begin with an affirmation of protection, stated mentally or out loud. <u>The intention to call on the spiritual force should always precede the practice of affirmation.</u> An example of a protection affirmation is this: *"In the <u>Name</u>, through the <u>Power</u>, and by the <u>Word</u> of (name of divinity), a wall of living flame is built around and about me and I give thanks for this great protection Now."* This affirmation is from a Franciscan mystic, John Laurence.

    b. Visualizing white light around oneself, or another person(s), will intensify your connection to the spiritual force and energetically send forth this positive energy toward another. Visualizing white light may be accomplished by mentally tracing the idea of white light around the body, or visualizing a spherical, egg-shape pattern, making certain that the white light also is completed around both the head and the feet. It is not by your power to see or visualize white light, or colors around another person that brings forth a response; it is your vibrations of good intention that summons the love vibration in a manner that brings forth the energy of blessings for yourself or for another.

4. **Formal affirmation practice.** Take the list of affirmations that you have chosen and start with affirmation number two

(the first one always being for protection). If possible, state the affirmation out loud. Never repeat by rote, but concentrate on the meaning, intention, and the thought expressed by the words and sentences. Restate the affirmation 4-6 times. Then decrease the volume with approximately the same number of repetitions. Continue through several stages until you are at a whisper level, and then culminate this practice of affirmations by a mental repetition, using the same approximate number of repetitions each time.

5. **Then proceed to the next affirmation** following the same pattern.

> An excellent discussion and instruction on the practice of affirmations, as well as a list of potent spiritualized affirmations is to be found in:
>
> *Scientific Healing Affirmations*
> by
> Paramahansa Yogananda
>
> This publication is available on-line through Self-Realization Fellowship at http://www.yogananda-srf.org/ and at many bookstores.

If you attend only to your desires in the outer world, you will finally come to a place in your own experience where you are confronted by the discouraging truth: outer reality has no lasting power to satisfy your deepest desires. The inability of most people to achieve lasting, continuous happiness is a testimony to the inadequacy of the outer world in meeting our true needs. The struggle and seeming futility for the majority of us in pursuing happiness is not based on personality and character defects. The world cannot supply that which your spiritual nature yearns for; this is a fundamental cause of deep unhappiness and dissatisfaction in most lives. Man is ever in the vibration of that spiritual call, yet often listens to the whispers of his unworthiness. This journey is about increasing your awareness of that spiritual call. You need to believe that you will hear and answer that call.

You have the ability to empower yourself and your life.

Know Thyself – Spirit is Shining Within You

Increased self-awareness leads to a greater participation in Spirit. The determination to better know your spiritual nature will lead to more self-awareness. If you assume that inherent in man's nature is the desire to pursue happiness, then the quest is to achieve that worthy purpose in a manner that empowers self-knowing. Do you desire to increase your awareness of your own consciousness and to feel more whole? As you relate more consciously with yourself, you will inevitably change how you relate with all life.

The expansion of the self into higher states of happiness and joy always results from greater participation in the spiritual light, the spiritual essence that underlies all creation. When the self is in flow with Spirit, the light of consciousness expands. This expansion always carries with it the potential to perceive the divinity within. At the same time, you may glimpse with greater clarity and greater understanding the divinity that exists in all life, and in others.

What "Gets in Your Way" in Pursuing Happiness?

If you assume your happiness is tied, in some manner, to your spiritual nature, you may feel encouraged to pursue more of Spirit. But if enduring happiness is connected to the highest positive vibration of Spirit, then why is it so difficult to feel and sustain happiness? You may be left wondering "Why is Spirit so elusive?" And if we are spiritual in nature, then what are the obstacles to manifesting and maintaining happiness? Some frequently heard possibilities:

- Life.
- Others.
- Ourselves.
- Adversity and the negative polarity in the duality of creation.
- Unexpected change over which we have no control.
- The conditions of Earth and the alignment of the stars.
- Negative projections of early experiences onto the present.
- Personal traits that imitate behaviors of significant others from childhood.
- Feelings of unworthiness and questions of deservedness.
- Bad habits.
- A compulsion towards sense gratification.
- Addiction.
- Confusion over who you truly are.
- A longing for, but a lack of clarity, about what constitutes happiness.
- Negative thought patterns ingrained by repetition.
- The habit of worry.
- A lack of understanding of the conflict between separated parts of yourself and lack of integration and dialogue between your two opposing natures.

The subject of happiness and our own intense interest in that "higher state" appears to be more complex than we might first imagine. It isn't the same for all of us, and it may not be the same for you at all times. The good news and the bad news is that sometimes we get exactly what we imagine and believe will bring us happiness. We experience that golden moment when our needs, wants, and desires have been fulfilled. Yet, still, like the girl burned by that slide, we remain discontented. We might even feel our imagined desires prove to just be a fickle, demanding mistress, or an unrelenting taskmaster that has subjugated us.

In these moments, we may feel a profound sense of aloneness or separateness. We may attempt to climb through dense clouds of discouragement that obscure our clarity. In these moments, if we listen to the silence, we may hear the whisper: "there is more." If we hear that call of the light, we may either interpret it to be an invitation to pursue new wants, needs, and desires or, perhaps, we may begin to wonder about the "more." We may even come to ask, "Who is the Whisperer promising us there is more?" Is it part of ourselves or external to ourselves? And what part of us is responding to the intuitive truth being whispered?

The answer is this: You—and all of us—have another self whose joy is in Being. This Self is knowable. But to understand this other self requires more effort and a willingness to accept that claiming happiness is difficult. The process of understanding this other, Higher Self, is one of the cornerstones of this book.

The nature, origin, orientation and activities of these two selves, one Limited, the other Eternal is the subject of the next chapter.

Affirmations for Happiness

For Sunshine from Behind the Clouds
Behind the clouds
sunlight shines.
Behind the trees
flowers grow.
Behind the gloom
joy hides.

For Alignment with the Power of Spirit
Celestial Light,
align me with the truth
of my essence and the
power of Spirit.

For Clear Perception in Consciousness
Clear perception is mine.
Contemplative awareness is mine.
My Interiorized Consciousness brings me peace.
My Interiorized Consciousness brings new joy.
My Interiorized Consciousness brings me bliss.

For Deliberate Happiness
Deliberate happiness is mine.
I am empowered
in the pursuit
and claiming
of my highest self.

For Co-creating Happiness NOW
I give thanks
for I am co-creating
my joy
and my happiness
in the NOW.

For Experiencing Joy and Peace
Joy and peace
ever new.
Joy and peace
ever new.
Joy and peace
ever new.

For Knowing I Am That
Joy bursts within me.
I know my name.
I am that.

For Joy In My Nature
Joy is my nature.
Peace sustains me.
Contentment is mine.
Joy is mine.

For Peace, Joy, and Love
Peace, Peace, Peace
ever deepening,
ever expanding.
Joy, Joy, Joy
ever deepening,
ever expanding.
Love, Love, Love
ever deepening,
ever expanding.

By Yvonne Christenson

CHAPTER TWO

OUR DUAL NATURE:
THE LIMITED SELF AND THE ETERNAL SELF

Whether you are aware of it or not, your silent, spiritual Self beckons you. Your desire for happiness is a response to a distant trumpet call summoning you homeward to Spirit.

KEY TOPICS ADDRESSED IN THIS CHAPTER ARE:
- Why we pursue happiness.
- Introduction and exploration of the Limited Self.
- Introduction and exploration of the Eternal Self.
- The conflict between these two selves.
- Limited Self's pursuit of happiness.
- Eternal Self's natural state of happiness and joy.
- Self-knowing tied to our spiritual journey.
- Meditation, visualization, and affirmations as bridges between the two selves.
- Integration of the Limited and Eternal Selves.
- Affirmations for Integration.

The Essence of Happiness

The subject of happiness is so profound that it is written about in the world's great literature as well as in its eminent spiritual traditions. The pursuit of happiness is a fundamental right, referenced in the U.S. Constitution. It is a driving force, which underlies our ventures and adventures in this physical world. Happiness also can be intensely consuming and powerful in and of itself.

But why do we pursue happiness? Is it simply a reflex effort to avoid pain, or is it a distinct drive to access a greater, higher state of pleasure? Is pleasure simply experienced at the physical and psychological levels, or could there be a state of transcendent pleasure that is tied to our spiritual nature? With a need so basic, so deeply intrinsic to our nature, why does it remain elusive?

Without understanding our dual nature, human and divine, our efforts to "find" happiness are misplaced. Happiness on the material level is transitory—a vanishing specter of possibility. The more we experience our true nature, however, the greater our experience of self-empowerment and then joy, our native state.

Our dilemma is that we have two opposing selves, in frequent communication and yet functioning in nearly opposite ways. This is not an abstract philosophical quandary; it is a pervasive reality. Our lack of conscious awareness of these two selves complicates our attempts to achieve peace, harmony, and happiness. Mankind's deepest expressions of philosophical and religious thought refer to this internal schism. Present-day author and psychologist John Welwood puts it succinctly: "To discover our human wholeness.... we need to bring the two sides of our nature – absolute and relative, supra-personal and personal, heaven and earth – together at last." This integration offers hope for healing the schism and finding inner peace and happiness.

The Two Selves Defined

It is helpful to discover what is true by distinguishing it from what is not true. The clearer we are, the greater our discernment with the often extremely subtle nuances of illusion. For this reason, let us take a deeper look at these two selves and how they operate in polarized consciousness. One, for the sake of this discussion, will be called the Limited Self, identified and bound by the physical form, mind, feelings and the culture in which it lives. The other, the Eternal Self, expresses our spiritual nature, our true unchangeable essence.

Put simply, the Limited Self consists of:

- Our chemical, biological nature, operating in the physical dimension under physiological laws.

- Our psychological layers of mental consciousness, operating within a social context.

- Our beliefs and life experiences, operating within our environment and culture.

> "Awakening is when the eyes of consciousness open so that consciousness begins to see what is real, instead of consciousness seeing only an illusion, or what it wants to be real."
>
> JOHN DE RUITER
> *Dialogues with Emerging Spiritual Teacher*

- Our extraordinary ability to evaluate, interpret and assign meaning to our experiences, literally defining ourselves through our imagination.

Because we seldom view the interface between these four aspects, our Limited Self may feel compartmentalized, incorrectly interpreting experiences and events, wrongly imagining ourselves as body identified, continuously changing, impermanent beings.

Even though the Limited Self is unaware of its spiritual potential, it nonetheless carries the capacity for joy within. However, fragmentation, conflict, and persistent habits of thought—including the habit of worry, circular negative thinking and defeating self-talk—become major impediments on our road to happiness and self-awareness.

Our other self, the expansive Eternal Self, is our true spiritual nature, pursuing nothing, for its state of consciousness is joy transcendent. That Self, our soul nature, is always aware of the actions and activities of the Limited Self. This spiritual essence manifests in subtle, powerful ways as the expression of who we truly are.

All physical life contains the movement of Divine Intelligence through the vibratory law of creation. As humans, we have an innate capacity to unfold through developmental stages into multi-faceted beings with highly advanced, complex thoughts, vivid imaginations, sparks of divine creativity and the ability to plan and achieve goals. Part of the miracle of our lives is that our magnificence in this form will never come again in exactly the same place, in the same way. Each of us is unique in the Universe. Our individual expression is unlike anyone else's.

Unfortunately, we generally go about life unaware of our infinite potential, for we are focused primarily on three-dimensional reality. We access knowledge through our bio-chemical nature and filter experiences through the individual persona, or ego. The five senses, as necessary as they are in helping us navigate this physical dimension, are like a twelve-inch ruler. They can measure the "fiber and texture" of the material world, but they cannot reach or measure Infinity.

> *The inner battle is between our lower self, or pseudo-self—the body identified ego—and our true higher self, the soul, the image of God within us.*
>
> PARAMAHANSA YOGANANDA

Relentless forces of change assault this Limited Self, for nothing stays the same in this world. Even the semi-permanent values and mores of the society are in a constant state of flux. As the world spins around us in an ever-changing panorama of experiences, our lives are impacted in ways great and small. Events happen, and we interpret and assign meaning to them. This capacity adds both to the wonder and the complexity to life. More often than not, our interpretation of events is subjective rather than objective. Fundamentally, we place a fog—a kind of conceptual overlay—onto our experiences and then make an emotional investment in that overlay, taking it to be "real" in and of itself.

We also have an innate ability to reflect on ourselves, a trait that lends resilience to our nature. Our ability to interpret and imagine can open a door to new interpretation and redefinition. We can restructure the meaning we see in the physical dimension. "Consciousness is imaginative, sensitive and pliable; it can think and dream itself into any state," wrote Indian scholar and sage, Paramahansa Yogananda. He is referring here to our amazing ability to re-create ourselves, to change and transform consciousness itself.

While the capacity for self-motivated change is always present, the Limited Self is more often changed by biological or psychological conditions that continually impact it. It is altered by the hands of circumstances and the clay of environment: childhood and our early upbringing, genetics, and diet are just a few of the influences that continually impact this Limited Self. With such a constant bombardment of uncertainty, where there is really no telling what may happen in the next moment, is there any wonder the Limited Self feels powerlessness against the law of change?

Stranger O' Self

*Stranger o' Self
Dream Self gone wandering
Among the ruins of time
Gone to find self meeting self
Yet strangers always.*

*Stranger o' Self
Viewed from countless mirrors
Reflectors of false images
Self seeing self
Distorted on a mirror of glass.*

*Unknown substance
in search of form.
Stranger, Dream Self
Gone wandering
Among the ruins of time.*

To operate entirely from the Limited Self makes the pursuit of happiness a precarious journey. "The only constant, is change," wrote the Greek philosopher Heraclitus. We do indeed live largely in a world of unending change over which none of us has true control.

But even in assessing ourselves through this limited, changeable self, we can continue to define and interpret. This is a deeply significant truth that will be reinforced throughout this book. In my counseling work through the years, I have seen clients, once awakened to their intrinsic capacity to choose new perspectives, come to reframe even the most difficult memories and experiences.

Until we claim that power to choose, and until that choosing comes from our more enlightened, expanded Eternal Self, our perceptions will be constrained by the Limited Self's view of reality. What we see, hear, sense, feel and therefore experience, is filtered through the mind with all its pre-conditioning. We begin to believe our thoughts and perceptions are real, regardless of their origin. Roger Walse, in his "State of the Integral Enterprise: Part 1," wrote: "What is crucial to recognize is that all perceptions reflect perspectives, and all perspectives are partial and selective. Each perspective both reveals and conceals, clarifies and distorts. However, perspectives and perceptions do not clearly reveal their own limitations."

Assumptions and perceptions can harden into beliefs, which can manifest, consciously or unconsciously, as behaviors. It is imperative, therefore, that we learn to recognize how this process of self-definition operates.

As long as limiting beliefs remain unknown and unconscious, we remain a puppet, pulled on the strings of conditioned behaviors or false concepts of ourselves. As a result, we will continue to experience a limited range of happiness. Fortunately, at our best, we naturally strive for the experience of knowing ourselves as integrated and whole.

> *Happiness is inherent in oneself and is not due to external causes. One must realize one's Self in order to open the store of unalloyed happiness.*
>
> RAMANA MAHARSHI

Personality is Ego-driven

Our personality, as delightful and creative as it may be, is limited to the perceptions of mind and body alone. Its drives are primarily based on preservation, survival, the elimination of pain, finding pleasure, and satisfying the senses, none of which, as we have seen, can provide true happiness. Nature intended for the ego-based personality to survive, reproduce, and endure. The emphasis of this ego-based personality is thus always upon the "I," which has little capacity to extend beyond itself to the needs, the necessities, the wants and desires of others.

Our human experience creates a kind of hypnosis in which we identify with the Limited Self. Jean Paul Sartre, the French existentialist, wrote: "Everything happens as if consciousness were hypnotized by this ego which it has established, which it has constructed, becoming absorbed in it as if to make the ego its guardian and law."

With this myopic view, the ego rarely sees beyond itself. Generally, the activities and drives of this ego-based personality do not allow for the stillness in which we can hear the call of the vastly subtler self. That other self, our soul nature, is ever in residence as we live in our physical-material reality. This self is hidden by the noise and drives of the world and our lack of attention to its existence.

Our Developmental Stages

Our entry into the material world as infants is driven foremost by the biology of survival. It is hardly a journey of mystical contemplation! From this beginning, the infant is on a journey of growing and expressing increased mastery of its biology. The developmental progression from birth at a physical and psychological level has definite patterns and transitions. Certain milestones of development that are age specific must occur if there is to be a normal physical and psychological growth and maturation.

Renowned psychoanalyst, Erik Erikson, addressed specifically the developmental stages and the areas of attempted psychological mastery that must occur in those specific stages. Piaget's classic work on children also shows us stages of child development using copious research, observation, and journey metaphors; he reveals this development through the eyes of the child, providing a clear view of the Limited Self's dominance in young human consciousness.

Our Dual Nature: The Limited Self and the Eternal Self

If a child grows with the proper guidance, developmental stages occur in proper sequence. These stages, however, are influenced by the interaction of parents, significant others, and the community in which the child lives. Through words, example and behaviors powerful messages are delivered to the child: these contribute to his own self-identification. The child receives both overt and covert messages; these have enormous potential for interpretation, adding to the intrigue and complexity of the youth's emotional and psychological journey.

> *What really has to (go) is our false self created by our own mind, ego, and culture. It is a pretense, a bogus identity, a passing fad, a psychological construct that gets in the way of who we are and always were.... This is the objective and metaphysical True Self.*
>
> RICHARD ROHR

The Limited Self is naturally rooted in this journey. Being human involves the physiological wiring of our nature in a physical world. By necessity, the child focuses on gaining greater skill over specific need areas, body mastery, and physical navigation in the world. This leads to body-based self-identification.

No wonder our self-esteem is reinforced by the idea that external mastery in the physical world is a natural source of happiness. So many messages in society reinforce this. Athletes become heroes; fashion models are idolized. Popularity is often based on glamour, wealth, and personality. Is it any wonder the young psyche can become confused?

The absorption and interpretation of messages, impressions, ideas, and verbalization create an experience of self-identity. There are not only layers upon layers of experience, but enmeshed layers of subtle reinforcement, and the co-mingling of these layers that create the masquerade of our "real self."

> "The ego feeling we are aware of now is… only a shrunken vestige of a far more extensive feeling – a feeling which embraced the universe and expressed an inseparable connection of the ego with the external world."
>
> SIGMUND FREUD

With the increasing capacity to contemplate, examine and verbalize one's experiences, the child feels that what we are calling the Limited Self is actually the core reality of his essence. Since the Limited Self must, of necessity, be identified with its biological journey and the physical, material world, it strives to access the world from this early core identification. The child seeks its happiness from the senses and the material world. Although the progressive formation of this Limited Self results in an undeniably real self, we are in truth, something vastly more complex, more wondrous.

Though most individuals abandon the ideas and desires of youth by changing or modifying them with experience, yet we still claim this Limited Self as solid and enduring even though the frailty of that perception can be seen in the reflecting mirror of changing experiences. One of the great delusive ideas posits the solidity and permanence of the Limited Self amidst impermanence and fragmentation.

The more we bring these distorted, fragmented areas to conscious awareness, the greater will be the possibility of integrating them. The greater the denial about opposing parts within us, the greater the potential that there will be conflict and a lack of personal integration. Denial and lack of self-knowledge perpetuate fragmentation and lessen our chances of experiencing continuous fulfillment and happiness.

Illusory Happiness

When asked to write down what we feel would give us happiness, many of us will naturally respond with answers centered on physical-material objects, or success in that realm. Some responses will be relationship-based or about love and happiness, generally. Often we believe that the possession of, or the constant access to another person is the source of our happiness. This is because the Limited Self does not fully understand that the desire to experience love is also an invitation to know more of the Eternal Self. Instead, it interprets love as a sensory or material experience associated with its own nature.

Happiness for the Limited Self has to be, in some way, tied to the experiences or desires of life in a physical body in a material world. In this state of being, our capacity for happiness is not only determined by our habitual state of mind, whether positive or negative, but by our emotional response to events. Emotions become charged with expectation and interpretation. This generally leads to replaying and reinterpreting along similar ideas or themes. Memory replay is again subject to interpretation. And off we go on a repetitive cycle that is difficult to break. Let's take a deeper look at how thought patterns work.

> *DNA is controlled by extra-cellular signals, including the energetic messages emanating from our positive and negative thoughts. By retraining our minds to create healthy beliefs, we can change the physiology of our trillion-celled bodies. Dr. Lipton's profoundly hopeful synthesis of the latest and best research in cell biology and quantum physics is being hailed as a major breakthrough in our awareness of how our cells, our bodies and our minds work.*
>
> BRUCE LIPTON
> *Biology of Belief*

How Habit Patterns are Formed

Our interpretations of events create energy. This blueprint energy creates grooves in our brains that allow for further movement of energy through which our consciousness travels. New experiences tend to gravitate into existing energy grooves. Once a particular thought groove is activated by a repetitive thought, a tendency is formed. It is extremely difficult to change the tendencies of the physical mind for so many of our thoughts are automatic and therefore unconscious.

In the last few decades, scientists have shown that we can change the structure and function of our brains by the way we think. This newly conceptualized feature of the brain is called neuroplasticity. For years, the conventional wisdom of neuroscience held that the hardware of the brain is fixed and immutable – that we are stuck with what we were born with. Yet *Wall Street Journal* science writer, Sharon Begley, reveals an entirely new paradigm in her book, *Train the Mind, Change the Brain*. She describes pioneering experiments in the field of neuroplasticity that investigate how the brain can undergo wholesale change. These experiments reveal that the brain is capable not only of altering its structure but also of generating new neurons, even into old age.

By the act of mental repetition, and the mental replay of ideas, we create new energy grooves. Our power to create new energy grooves means we have the power to recreate, re-imagine, and re-energize any event that occurred in the physical-material world.

We stand at a crossroads with every experience in life from smelling a flower to failing an exam at school, dealing with a promotion to falling in love or coping with a major loss. How we interpret the experience determines our reality and sets up the blueprint for similar experiences in the future. Our interpretive capacity crystallizes these perceptions in a manner that either integrates or fragments us, creating harmony or dissonance. The repetition of these ideas forges self-identity and creates energy grooves and memory grooves in the physiology of the brain itself.

The repetition of these themes can lead to either positive or negative self-talk. The more energy and repetition on any theme, the greater the energy grooves available for that theme. And the deeper and more pronounced the energy groove, the more likely that there will be a tendency toward similar interpretations. The late self-help author Robert Collier put it this way: "One comes to believe whatever one repeats to oneself sufficiently often, whether the statement be true or false. It comes to be the dominating thought in one's mind." It is imperative, therefore, that we become more aware of our habitual trends of thought.

Confusion can result when we place too much emphasis on our interpretations of events, experiences and interactions. These interpretations are simply the movement of energy in chemical, biological and energy fields. They are not the true reflectors of reality. The habit of repeating ideas may help us feel solid. We may mistake that "solidity" for who we are. Ultimately, that is an illusion. We are more than our biology, interpretations, emotions, and habits of thought!

The Role of Psychology

Most self-help books are based on the premise that to achieve happiness or peace, we must better understand and master our psychological underpinnings.

But it is *only* the Limited Self that can achieve greater self-understanding through psychological approaches to self-discovery. This is a worthy endeavor, of course, for introspection, self-examination, and self-analysis are helpful tools in the process of knowing ourselves. Psychology is about the journey of consciousness, addressing as well the physiological aspects and their impact on consciousness. But if the consciousness of the Limited Self becomes the only area of investigation, the discovery of a larger, spiritual Self will be sacrificed and with it, the attainment of true integration.

We need to find the middle path. Bypassing the Limited Self in our efforts to access our spiritual self will not bring freedom and happiness anymore than the reverse. Buried or unresolved psychological issues will continue to fester if left unaddressed. The Limited Self is fertile soil for doing deep inner work. Without that work, those issues remain and will spring up as we delve more deeply into our spiritual nature. John Welwood speaks to this in his *Toward a Psychology of Awakening:* "As awareness starts to move beyond the boundaries of the conditioned personality structure, this expansion inevitably challenges that structure, flushing out old, subconscious, reactive patterns that often emerge with a vengeance."

When these reactive patterns are flushed to the surface, psychology can be a helpful therapeutic tool. However, its value, in general, is not the territory and the analysis of the spiritual nature of man. Psychological assistance from the hands of trained professionals gives us an invaluable gift. It is the gift of greater knowledge and the possibility of understanding more of ourselves, our journey, and the movement of our own consciousness. Yet, any lasting transformation of human consciousness ultimately has to provide the unshakable realization that we are at our core, spiritual beings, possessing an unchangeable nature rooted in joy.

Introducing the Eternal Self

Beyond the Limited Self is another Self, constant, changeless, integrated, unbounded by physiology, unaffected by alternating psychological states, impervious to societal or cultural influences. It functions by intuition, free of interpretation and faulty self-definition.

This Eternal Self is not searching for happiness because it already exists in the state of unalterable joy intrinsic to our very being. Our drive for happiness is not simply the thrust of our desire for self-gratification or for pleasure at a biological level. Rather, it is the spiritual call to a vision of ourselves that is often obscured by the seeming reality of the material world.

What if, in the search to discover who we are, we should find this expansive, radiant self underneath the layers of personality and material identifications? How would we experience it? Many of the world's spiritual traditions describe this self as the essence of Spirit, manifesting in creation through the vibratory energy of love and light. Though we may not consciously be aware of this self, it is nevertheless real and truly who we are. While we experience life as physical beings, this self remains profoundly separate, yet powerfully a part of us, immutable, unchangeable, enduring, permanent. This self is the expression of our soul nature. Here is a poem I wrote about this essential Self:

Forever More I Shall Be

I am
I am that which is
I am that which will always be.

I am immutable
I am the fortress
I am beyond all destruction.

I am deathless
I withstand all
For I am all.

When the world and the universe of matter
Shall crumble, I shall remain serene!
When the sun shall fall from the heavens
My light shall light the world of worlds!

When I shed forevermore my forms
I shall be with form
And yet formless!

For I am
And forever more I shall be!

> *Being is not only beyond but also deep within every form as its innermost invisible and indestructible essence. This means that it is accessible to you now as your own deepest self, your true nature....You can know it only when the mind is still. When you are present, when your attention is fully and intensely in the Now.*
>
> ECKART TOLLE

The Higher Self is Spirit experimenting and participating in the journey of being human. If this is so, how, then, might we find greater happiness, especially if the essence of our being is already joy itself? Perhaps joy undiscovered, perhaps peace uncultivated, but nevertheless in the purest sense that eternal joy exists. If that is true, then the art of finding true happiness lies in accessing and empowering who we truly are, spiritual beings who are also living a physical-material journey. Without the journey inward, we may find that lasting happiness is always just beyond our grasp. *It is a journey requiring deep commitment to self-discovery, and steadfast patience, as the Irish saying goes, the "patience that can conquer destiny."*

The Well of Silence Within

Meditation has been used through the centuries as a method for acquiring spiritual self-knowledge. It is based on the idea that as the consciousness becomes interiorized, we have more access to our essence or true nature. "Be still and know that I am God" conveys this truth with simple clarity. The silence of meditation is not just a passive quietness. It embodies a dynamic and vast consciousness far beyond our usual experience. In this mental stillness, we can access our own hidden consciousness.

Real empowerment must include the cultivation of a relationship with your truest self, the Eternal Self, which rests in the center of your being. This Self begins to emerge when you peel away the layers of ego consciousness through meditation, introspection and other awareness-based practices. All beings, no matter how reactionary, fearful, violent or lost, can open themselves to the sacred within and become free. Spirit is your very being. Meditation allows you access to the deeper regions of your spiritual nature, connects you with the Divine presence within, and provides us a clearer vision of the truth. Scheduling time each day for meditation practice is essential not only for peace and well being and empowerment, but for experiencing your Eternal Self, the true source of lasting happiness. There are countless meditation techniques available and myriad philosophies about the proper method of meditation. Finding an effective and suitable style of meditation can take time and experimentation but will prove invaluable. One technique is offered below.

Meditation Technique

The proper posture for meditation is very important.

- Sitting in a straight back chair is recommended.
- The feet should be flat on the floor, pointed straight ahead.
- In a state of relaxation, maintain a straight spine, to the best of your ability without straining or discomfort.
- Place your hands, with palms turned gently upward, near the junction between your legs and thighs.

(Note: Meditation techniques, in general, should not be practiced in a position where the individual is lying down in a bed. When lying down, the meditative state too easily becomes a sleep state. If an individual has the physical ability to sit either in a chair with feet flat on the floor—or cross-legged on the floor on a flat surface, the sitting posture should be assumed. In general avoid sitting on a bed, for consciousness usually associates the bed with sleep.)

This meditation technique involves focusing your attention at the point between the eyebrows known as the "spiritual eye." This is a center that increases our spiritual connectedness as we focus upon it. If you are having difficulty in achieving or maintaining the proper eye position for your meditation, the following suggestion may assist you in getting the correct angle for your focus gaze. The eyes should be turned gently and slightly upward.

Pencil Technique for Proper Gaze

Visualize holding a #2 pencil eraser at the spiritual eye. Visualize the eraser resting on the forehead between and slightly above the eyebrows, centered at the spiritual eye, with the pencil parallel to the ground. Allow your focus to move to where you visualize the point of the pencil to be. Keep the gaze focused at that spot. This technique is not part of the practice itself, but will prevent you from placing excessive strain on the eyes and help develop a better habit pattern for meditation.

Note: There should be no strain or tension. This is a natural, pleasant position for the eyes.

Preparation for Meditation:

- Visualize that you are encircled by white light which either outlines the body or appears as a spherical egg-shape. It is the <u>intention</u> to place white light around the body that summons a greater connection with Spirit and strengthens the energy field.

- After visualizing the white light in this way, begin to observe the breath in a relaxed state of mind. Maintain the correct posture with spine erect and feet flat on the floor.

- Affirm that the surrounding white light of Spirit divinely protects you. (Example: "I am surrounded by the light field of the Divine. I am ever protected. I am ever embraced by the Divine Force.") Repeat this protection affirmation, or a similar one, between 12-16 times.

Our Dual Nature: The Limited Self and the Eternal Self

- Now, in this relaxed state of mind, begin to observe the breath without any attempt to regulate it. Neither speed up nor slow down the rhythm of the breath. Simply observe the inhalation and exhalation as it naturally flows in and out.

- See yourself as "piggy-backing" on each inhalation and exhalation. Mentally say, "I ride the inward breath." As you naturally begin to exhale, mentally say, "I ride the outward breath." Continue this pattern for approximately 15 minutes. Visualize yourself riding the inward breath and the outward breath. Then change the repetition of words on the inhaling and exhaling breath to "I am That[1]".

Additional affirmations that may be mentally repeated prior to or following the use of this meditation technique:

I ride the inward breath.
I ride the outward breath.
I am one with that breath.
Reveal Thyself,

Note: Effective meditation techniques are available from Self-Realization Fellowship in the form of lessons that are delivered to your home every two weeks.

For information contact:

Self-Realization Fellowship
3880 San Rafael Drive
Los Angeles, CA 90065-3219
323-225-2471
http//www.yogananda-srf.org

---

[1] "I am That" refers to our being One with the Indwelling Spirit.

Such techniques of will-charged visualization and spiritualized affirmation are also powerful conduits and conveyors of truth that promote access to this highest self. The irony is that our spiritual, expansive, all-knowing self is never in pursuit of its own happiness. Its nature is already joy, peace, and bliss. In its silence, it is summoning the Limited Self into a greater alliance with itself. In the Greek myth, Narcissus falls in love with his own image reflected in a still pool of water. In a spiritual interpretation, he may be seeing the truth of his own divine nature reflecting back in the still waters.

While this reflection is generally obscured, there is nevertheless a powerful drive within us not only to perceive our true image, our true Self, but to become fully one with it. We desire the joy that is more than an extension of the happiness of the earth. Seemingly just out of reach, we tend to fall back on our belief in the tangible self of change and vacillating, unstable circumstances. We may operate on the myth that this kaleidoscope of images is our true self and that if we can run fast enough, we will catch and possess ourselves and achieve a state of unchanging happiness. Like the proverbial dog chasing its own tail, we go round and round in search of something that is already within us.

True access lies in the stillness and the subtleties of the movement of Spirit. Eckart Tolle wrote: "Your innermost sense of self, of who you are, is inseparable from stillness. This is the I Am that is deeper than name and form." His words are an invitation to a voyage of self-discovery. They invite our activity-driven mind and sense identification to move past the pursuits of the world, toward calmness, serenity, peace, tranquility, and self-knowing beyond any definition. This is where deep meditation will take us.

For those who believe that in time they will possess happiness because of the nature of their dreams and goals, the world offers strong encouragement to continue to pursue that pathway. Nothing that another may say will alter the momentum of that journey. For those who doubt that the world in and of itself will be able to provide happiness, know that such perceptions can be clarified. Doubt can be a catalyst for us to seek deeper, thus creating a bridge to a new level of integration between the two selves.

The tools of meditation, visualization and affirmation are the bridge-builders for the fragmented parts of our Limited Self. To achieve true, lasting happiness, the self of the world must come into alliance, alignment and attunement with the Divine aspect of the self.

Characteristics of the Limited Self and Eternal Self

Limited Self	Eternal Self
Ego-driven consciousness	Spirit-based consciousness
Identifies with the body and the material world	Not subject to identification with body, senses or material pleasures
Biological and psychological identification is foundational	Spirit in man beyond all definition
Shaped by experiences and interpretations of those experiences	Immutable, absolute in being
Resides in our genetic heritage	Independent of genetic heritage
Desires to seek and possess happiness	Never in pursuit of its own happiness; continually joyful
Progresses through an innate developmental pattern of psychological and biological stages	Manifests in creation through the vibratory energy of love and light
Impacted and changed by circumstances and faulty self-definition	Not impacted by changing conditions or circumstances
Struggles with feelings of powerlessness against the Law of Change	Changeless nature is constant joy, peace, bliss
Ever changing and unstable due to circumstances, with illusion of control	Has enduring permanence, unfaltering truth, vibratory consistency with spirit
Happiness associated with fulfillment of biological drives and gratification	Happiness inherent in being independent of external desires

Affirmations to Help Integrate Your Dual Nature

For Integration
Attuned, Aligned,
Integrated Self
Content in Being,
Peaceful in Serenity,
Awake in Spirit.

For Joy-filled Bliss
Being in knowing
I am.
Joy-filled,
light-illuminated,
ever penetrated,
ever known.
Joy-filled bliss I am.
Joy-filled bliss I am.

For Becoming One with the Light
I am the Light
of all suns.
I possess the power
of all creations.
My name is the name
of all Light,
all suns,
all power,
and all creations.

For Seeing My Face in God
I behold the face of God.
I parted the curtains of penetration
and the face I saw
was my own.

For Becoming One with All That Is
In becoming one
with nature
I claim my
nature.
I am Spirit
in nature.

For Silent Discovery
In silence,
the seeker finds
himself.

For Intentional Focus
Intentioned focus increases my power
of concentration.
In concentration
I perceive the whole,
and the parts,
moving in perfected
harmony.

Our Dual Nature: The Limited Self and the Eternal Self

For Greater Purified Consciousness
Oh Lord, may I become less of myself
in ego-based consciousness
that I may become ever more one with Thee.
May I become truly a purified conduit
of Your love, of Your light, of Your grace.

For Becoming a Mirror of the Divine
May I become a perfected mirror
of the divine essence
which is You, Oh Lord.

By Jacqui Freedman

CHAPTER THREE

Empower The Now

By greater engagement with your inner life, you will come to higher states of self-realization as you discover the infinite within and touch the face of God.

KEY TOPICS ADDRESSED IN THIS CHAPTER ARE:
- Cultivating self-love and loving others.
- Liking yourself.
- Using the serenity prayer – a living philosophy of life.
- Reframing and claiming.
- Achieving even-mindedness, your compass for the journey.
- Addressing spirituality as an aspect of empowerment.
- Viewing yourself as Spirit on a physical journey.
- Distinguishing between religion and spirituality.
- Removing obstacles and resistance to spiritual realization.
- Using intention to increase spiritual awareness.
- Increasing your experience in direct-knowing.

- Making spiritual effort.
- Cultivating the authentic voice.
- Meditation and affirmations to develop that voice.
- Exploring consciousness.
- Teaching and mentoring.
- Embracing the gifts of "I".
- Living in the present.
- Spiritual power.
- Hearing the voice of the other.
- Potent power thoughts.

Empowerment: Your Bedrock

Achieving a sense of empowerment means making yourself a creative actor in your own life. When you live an empowered life, you live a more loving life—in the Here and Now in connection with Spirit. Yet so many themes and emotions interfere with the ability to feel empowered, to pursue happiness and to know who you truly are.

You may identify so powerfully with the body and mind as you perceive them or attach so powerfully to ideas about what happiness will look like that you may feel you are grasping mist as you live mentally in the past and the future instead of the Now. The left part of your brain interprets your story, but this highly dynamic "Spin Doctor" is grooved with themes of lack of worthiness and deservedness and presents distorted mirrors of your true self. And so, in your search for greater empowerment, just as in other areas covered in this book, you need to look at the obstacles to knowing yourself and pursuing happiness.

Your habits in consciousness are a major deterrent to experiencing peace, happiness and joy. But you can frame and reframe experiences and employ journaling and meditation as steps on the path toward true empowerment, both personal and spiritual. Once more, you may have to explore your ideas about whether there is one self defined by its identification and the body and its material realm, an identification that may block your discovery of the real self. You may need again to clarify "Who is it *really* that journeys in this life."

Such ideas and discussions are required not only to explore your empowerment, but also to claim it! Empowerment does not mean acquiring power, but rather understanding the inner power that is radiant in its potency to create, inspire, shine and materialize. That inner power beckons you to own it and radiate it.

This chapter also continues to invite you to the stillness of meditation and the use of affirmations to expand your own powerful creativity. You have the ability to create new universes by shifting your habits in consciousness, and to reach the cavern of peace by taking small steps in your meditations. Meditation and affirmations help weaken your identification with the physical body and mind, the Limited Self. You are infinitely more than that—Spirit itself on an earthly journey, empowered to know your true self and to create deliberate happiness.

As you explore various facets of empowerment in this chapter, you will see that it is the bedrock of all you wish to accomplish in life. Empowerment comes from your innermost self, an inner presence and perspective that rises from a feeling of security and knowing deep within. This "knowing" is the sacred connection between your inner being and Spirit, a sense of personal power that stands strong in the face of adversity. When you are empowered, you may be shaken at times, but you are not deterred. Like the mythical Phoenix, your empowered self will pull you out of the ashes of despair and helplessness.

How is self-empowerment born? Where do you find it? You begin by taking small steps, the first of which is to accept responsibility for your life—your thoughts, actions, relationships, and consciousness. Ultimately, no one has dominion over you. You recognize that you must create your own happiness instead of being passive and leaving your happiness in the hands of others. This inner dynamism and resolve sets you on the path of awakening an abiding sense of empowerment that will travel with you throughout life. Each step strengthens you and gives you greater confidence. Each step takes you toward becoming an empowered creator of deliberate happiness.

Empowerment is a Mental Attitude

Empowerment is the natural outcome of a positive attitude. It involves a core belief in life and in your capacity to rise triumphant, regardless of circumstances. You may not have made all the right choices in life. You may have stumbled and made mistakes and misjudgments. When you are empowered, however, you have an unshakable knowing inside that you are bigger than your trials, that you can change and create a better, more fulfilling life.

Personal empowerment evolves out of your philosophy toward life, at the center of which is your relationship with yourself. A strong belief in yourself and a positive viewpoint about life are necessary for happiness, fulfillment and success; they go hand in hand. With them you feel that you are stronger than your circumstances, can create your own destiny and deserve every good thing.

This strong conviction in yourself can give you a higher degree of openness and willingness to achieve self-knowledge. You become less inclined toward self-deception. You want to know the truth about areas in your life that must change, even transform. This healthy, honest, open attitude allows you to be responsible for your thoughts, feelings and actions.

False Core Thoughts

Thoughts and behaviors are your compass on this inner journey. By observing them you can determine if you are headed "due north" toward contentment and happiness or in another direction altogether.

If you are not happy, you need to reconsider your thoughts, feelings and behaviors. Beneath discontent and powerlessness there often lurk hidden beliefs about your inability to effect true change. Do you ever say to yourself: "I am unable to change my life?" If the answer is yes, you need to uncover why this judgment exists. These and similar thoughts can be paralyzing. That is why it is so important to journal each day to become more conscious of how you undermine yourself. To transform your life you must become aware of the obstacles to your efforts.

> *Within each of us is a hidden store of energy. Energy we can release to compete in the marathon of life. Within each of us is a hidden store of courage, courage to give us the strength to face any challenge. Within each of us is a hidden store of determination, determination to keep us in the race when all seems lost.*
>
> ROGER DAWSON
> *13 Secrets of Power Performance*

Here are some examples of self-defeating thoughts/beliefs:

- I am the victim of forces and circumstances beyond my control.
- I am a victim of my past.
- I have missed my opportunities.
- When good things happen in my life, they never last.
- I will always be limited because negative things happened to me.
- Nothing that I do will make a difference.
- It's too late for me to change.
- I can't move beyond the hurt that I feel.
- I look in on my life from the outside, not being there.
- I try to change my bad habits, but I always go back.

- I lack the willpower to change.
- Other people have good luck and good fortune, not me.

Everything You Need Lies Within

> *By choosing your thoughts, and by selecting which emotional currents you will release and which you will reinforce, you determine the quality of your Light. You determine the effects that you will have upon others, and the nature of the experiences of your life.*
>
> GARY ZUKAV
> *Seat of The Soul*

None of us consciously wants to be unhappy, powerless, discouraged or disempowered. We are beings of Light, capable of enormous accomplishments – unbounded creativity, joy, love. You can further your own personal empowerment; you deserve and are entitled to it! When you commit to change, and follow through on that commitment, you alter the possibilities of the universe. In that altering, you change what will be attracted to you by the law of magnetism. When you make positive change, the frequency of your energy field is activated to attract new conditions and new circumstances. Your life, your circumstances, and the energy field around you are magnetized by your efforts and intentions in subtle yet powerful ways. You begin to co-create with the Divine. Because your divine essence is within, it is contrary to your nature to see yourself as a slave or sinner. You are an initiator and co-producer of your life's drama because you are a child of God.

All Conditions Can Be Transformed

Nothing exists that cannot be changed by divine energy. You can harness and project thoughts which are the energy waves of the universe. Your thoughts do alter the vibratory frequency of matter; you are not in singular control of that energy, but can influence it by directing your thoughts, will and intention in the fields of light. The entire universe is consciousness and consists of various rates of vibration. Everything and everyone vibrates at a certain frequency. Thoughts and emotions also vibrate as electromagnetic waves. In this way, your thoughts and emotions actually shape your material reality. You create your world all the time, consciously or unconsciously.

What gets in the way of seeing yourself as a powerful being capable of change? What ideas block your ability to access your power? One of the most devastating beliefs may be that you are powerless to change. This sense of impotence, however obvious or subtle, can lead to feelings of hopelessness and despair. When you take back your power from these false thoughts, you will feel a tremendous surge of hope and positive energy. Creativity flows and you are charged with a new determination to achieve your dreams and goals.

Cultivating Self Love

To express, expand, and embrace your I-ness, stretch your arms and wrap them tenderly around yourself.

Nurturing your relationship with yourself is empowerment in action. Energized intention vibrates with force and intensity when invigorated by the love vibration. So the place to begin expanding your love is with yourself. You are "true" to yourself when you learn to love, cherish and honor your own heart and the attributes that make you who you truly are. Only out of this self-love can you truly love others.

Most of us agree, at least theoretically, that we need to love ourselves. But do you *live that love* in your innermost thoughts, feelings and behaviors? Let's take a closer look at how you can take the concept of self-love and make it a powerful daily affirmation that permeates your life.

- When you love yourself unconditionally, you place no limits on how to behave or how to be in order to accept yourself.
- Self-love ignores "if-then" clauses that establish conditions for accepting and loving yourself.
- You accept and love yourself because you exist rather than for what you do.
- Empowerment begins and ends with self-love.
- Self-acceptance is an act of self-loving.
- You contain creation itself; creativity and power must exude from within. Lovingly embrace that concept of self.
- Celebrate yourself as a conveyor of light, a generator of possibilities, and a divine expression of the Infinite.
- By developing greater self-love there is a greater alignment between the Limited and Eternal Selves.

The following poem expresses the truth about your self and every human being, that you are a Gift.

The Gift of You

You are condensed starlight,
the sun and the moon of the universe.
You are a creator of divine sparks and emanations.
You are a carrier of the keys to the universe.

In your touch, hope awakens.
In your words, the sun shines brighter.
In your prayers, the moon softens the night.
And in your living, all the stars shine,
Awakened from their sleep by your desires for knowing
and because you are.

Going Deeper: Journaling Questions

- How do you feel about the idea that the first love relationship to be cultivated is the love for yourself? Why would this be true?
- Do you see yourself as lovable, worthy, and empowered?
- Do you see loving yourself as a valid goal? Or, do you feel self-love is egotistical?
- Do you feel you deserve love and are worthy of being loved?
- If someone said, "you have a lovable nature," what comes to mind?
- Do your ideas of love revolve primarily around romance and a physical relationship?
- What emotions do you feel when you hear "love yourself"?
- Do you feel a deep sense of peace and contentment about your worth and identity? Or, do you look for validation from others?
- Have you transferred any of your power to another, or a cause, trying to get self-validation?
- Is some person or cause a higher priority than cultivating the relationship with yourself? In the name of "duty" or "role expectation," have you surrendered parts of yourself?
- Are you comfortable with yourself in silence as well as in the company of others? Are silence and stillness foreign ideas?
- Have you embraced the idea that self-love originates from a deepening understanding of your own nature?

When you journal to answer these questions, you may uncover deep, previously unrecognized beliefs and pre-conditioning. Eric Fromm in his seminal *Escape from Freedom* talks about our ability to transfer our power to people, political causes, relationships, organizations, in an effort to escape our aloneness. Any interesting discoveries?

What is Self-Love?

Without self-love, there can be no empowerment, for love emanates from the Source of all Life and Power and is at the core of your being. Self-love means seeing yourself with all your flaws, talents, strengths and failings, and knowing, deep down, that you are lovable. You are an inseparable part of the Divine Love and Intelligence in all things. True self love arises from a sacred relationship with the Infinite, from which we all come.

Self-knowing involves personal spiritual expansion in the vibration of love. Not an intellectual acquisition, self-love is the actualization of consciousness which allows you to penetrate into divine energy. Some may feel uncomfortable with this topic as it seems to imply being overly self-involved. However, self-love is not about exalting the personality or ego-based self; rather it is the state of consciousness that emanates from greater awareness of the Eternal Self. This awareness sees the oneness of all things and naturally extends to others. From this consciousness, you feel sympathy and empathy for others. Compassion for the human condition flows deeply and genuinely from the Eternal Self.

Steps Toward Self Love

Personal and spiritual empowerment requires not only greater contact with your spiritual dimension, but mastering the art of *liking* your human self. You can begin to develop this attitude by writing down at least five things you like about yourself, and why. You can also write down things other people like about you and why. What positive feedback have you received? It is a wonderful exercise in self-affirmation to keep a list of all the qualities you genuinely "like" about yourself.

Any lack of self-love creates internal discord. If you don't really like yourself much, that negative sentiment will run beneath the sands of your life and eventually erode your efforts to claim love and happiness. Unconditional self-acceptance, with appreciation and compassion for yourself, is the foundation of empowerment. To love yourself is to love your essence, to see it as worthy of all good. So powerful is our need to love ourselves that lack of love can lead to illness. Abraham Maslow, the renowned psychiatrist, wrote of this: "If the essential core of the person is denied or suppressed, he gets sick, sometimes in obvious ways, sometimes in subtle ways, sometimes immediately, sometimes later."

Your self-empowerment is a precious treasure intrinsically connected to the Source of all love, wisdom and divinity. To access it is to access the vibrational energy and essence of love. You cannot think or will your way there. You must attune your consciousness by greater alignment between the two selves. Then you may enter the stream of love that eventually becomes a surging reservoir of joy, peace and bliss.

> *Self-love is above all a spiritual matter. For it is only when we can actually see and feel ourselves as one of the threads in the vast human shawl, as deeply, indeed, unconditionally received by a passionately caring and beautifully ordered universe, that we can truly love ourselves. This true, felt sense of ourselves as a precious part of the universe is really the ultimate source from which we can love others.*
>
> DAPHNE ROSE KINGMAN
> *Loving Yourself: Four Steps to a Happier You*

God is Love; You are Love, Light, and Spirit. True Empowerment and Happiness Depends Upon Your Deeper Penetration into This Truth.

As you progress on your journey of self-love, you begin to shed unnecessary psychological defenses. These defenses are no longer needed to shield the psyche or ego-based consciousness. You become more transparent, and a profound simplicity enters into your being, for no longer do you spend energy defending yourself. Self-knowledge brings freedom from the tyrannical control of ego-based needs.

In India, the sages have a saying "Ever fed, never satisfied" referring to the nature of the Limited Self and its appetite. The more you give it, the more demanding and less satisfied it becomes. All of us, in some manner, live life from the perspective of the Limited Self. In that state, knowing is always filtered through ego-based sense identification with the world. The ideal goal of the Limited Self in reference to deepening self-love is to lessen the ego-based filter and experience more of the divine interior.

Perceived separation from source is the basis of all experiences of fear and insufficiency. True empowerment means cultivating your relationship with the Eternal Self resting in the center of your being. This Self begins to emerge when we peel away layers of ego consciousness through meditation, introspection and other mindful practices such as:

1. Enhancing self-awareness by observation, introspection, and self-dialogue, as well as journaling.
2. Increasing conscious efforts to be more aware of others.
3. Praising yourself, and your efforts, more generously, lavishly, and consistently.
4. Eliminating negative self-talk by greater awareness and vibrant words of truth in affirmations.

These efforts create a bridge over which you can move from a smaller, more confined awareness toward the expansive nature of Spirit. You can gauge your progress when you begin to notice you are valuing and honoring yourself more in your thoughts, feelings and behavior. Self-observation is the key.

Empowerment, Humility and Self-Love

Some people feel that "to love oneself" suggests pride and a lack of humility, even irreverence toward Spirit. True humility means to understand that God is Doer, and that you are part of that infinite actor and action. To honor that truth is to express self-love. True humility acknowledges that the small self is not the creator of all though it is tied powerfully, intricately, and magnificently to the Source of all.

Self-love and the Limited Self

When looking through the "lens" of the Limited Self you may view self-love with the egotistical tendencies of the smaller self. As you know, ego-based self-absorption and narcissism are not self-love. They are distortions. Self-love, tied to the Limited Self, expresses itself in the wants, needs, and desires of the ego. Such ego-based desires create a tendency to justify the means used to fulfill those desires. This type of self-focus can become exploitation, an "all's fair in love and war" mentality, with people viewed as disposable commodities.

A lack of reverence for life may also develop as the ego seeks material success, no matter the cost to others. This "business is business" mentality ignores the impact on other people's personal lives or businesses. Yet corporate enterprises do not exist independently of the human spirit. This disdain for consequences equates self-love with self-gratification.

By contrast, true self-love connects the Limited Self and the Eternal Self.

Empowerment, Self-love and the Eternal Self

Self-love in reference to the Eternal Self is beyond ego-identification and individual personality. The opinions of others, as well

> *Until he extends his circle of compassion to include all living things, man will not himself find peace.*
>
> ALBERT SCHWEITZER

as your own distorted self-perception, cannot alter the knowing of the Eternal Self. The Eternal Self is accessed by penetration into pure being. Techniques to interiorize consciousness, such as meditation, can allow you to more fully experience peace and awareness of your deeper dimensions. As you deepen your connection with your Eternal Self you become increasingly purified by the light and consciousness of Spirit.

The Spiritual Journey into True Empowerment Involves an Increase in Self-knowing and Self-loving.

No agendas underpin self-love when it radiates from the Eternal Self. It is a love without bias, without prejudice, and without a diminished view of self or others. Such self-love is based on direct perception, clarity in knowing, and experience in being. Self-love is unconditional. It vibrates with the empathic heart of God. It validates the connection of all souls to one another. All is one! The human struggle is seen as part of a process, a journey. Judgment of self and others is modified by that awareness. Preconceptions and judgments are the territory of the Limited Self and not the Eternal Self.

Self-love from this perspective is expansive and universal in its ramifications. When your sense of self is exalted, your perception of your personal power and the worth of others are simultaneously enhanced. You cannot increase your awareness of yourself in self-love without that vibration including others. This is a significant distinction from the experience of the Limited Self which is preoccupied primarily with itself. The Eternal Self penetrates into spiritual nature which is all-inclusive.

Experiencing the Eternal Self

You cannot grasp the nature of the Eternal Self all at once. You must begin with small steps. Your intention to become more self-aware will motivate greater self-examination. With self-examination you are better able to integrate the Limited and the Eternal Self. The goal is not the annihilation of the Limited Self. It is a re-ordering of the relationship between the Eternal Self in consciousness over the narrow perspective of the Limited Self.

> *Everything you need you already have. You are complete right now, you are a whole, total person, not an apprentice person on the way to someplace else. Your completeness must be understood by you and experienced in your thoughts as your own personal reality.*
>
> — WAYNE DYER

As you increasingly connect with your innermost being, self-love expands, and you begin to experience peace, joy, and ultimately bliss. It is a long journey to that state of realization, but it is a journey that you can successfully complete. Your intention, well placed, takes you on that road to discovery, integration, self-knowing and self-loving in the experience of your Eternal Self.

The journey to experience that pure self-love requires your deepest commitment. At its heart is the search for your true nature as Spirit moving in the physical realm. You penetrate into it, not by faith alone, but by direct experience of awareness. The discovery of who you are as an eternal being awaits. You are a unique expression of divine individuality, moving through time and space. You we are not separate from God, nor prideful, nor inharmonious; you are love and light moving through the fields of light. This is the highest form of Self-realization.

A Comparison of Self-love from the Perspectives of the Limited Self and the Eternal Self

Limited Self	Eternal Self
Finite perspective	Infinite perspective
Consciousness of small self	Consciousness of true Self
Driven by wants, needs and desires	Unaffected by wants, needs and desires
Energy may be restrictive and lacking	Energy is expansive love
Ownership consciousness around things and others	No ownership consciousness around things and others
Happiness is transitory and unable to be sustained over time	Joy is ever increasing. Joy becomes ever new joy.
Consciousness of separateness from Source	Consciousness of existence within
Self knowing is subject to imagination, perception and interpretation	Self-knowing is direct perception of truth
Limited in knowing its nature	Unlimited in knowing its nature
Cognition in knowing	Cognition in being
Self-knowing is subject to change	Self-knowing is not subject to change
Limited Perception of self	Unlimited perception of Self

Spirituality

True empowerment at a personal level can only last if you turn your attention to cultivating the spiritual dimension. What does "spirituality" mean to you? Does it denote a highly organized structure such as a specific religious denomination? Perhaps it includes the concept of God or a Universal Force? "Spirituality" may even create a negative emotional reaction within you? Why? Perhaps you would be more comfortable acknowledging the spiritual dimension by entertaining a concept of your Higher Self, or Eternal Self? Try to give yourself permission to expand this dimension without having to align with dogmas or belief systems.

Many deny the spiritual aspect of themselves because of a negative experiences with institutional religion or with individuals who profess to believe in a certain religion. Look at any such negative experiences with religion by recording how you feel about words such as "God," "religion," "spirituality," the higher/Eternal Self." Journal about the words and feelings you associate with religion or spirituality. Can you identify previous efforts that involved looking at your spiritual nature more closely? Can you identify areas of resistance?

To increase your spirituality means to intensify your awareness of Spirit in man, and man in Spirit. Spirituality involves awakening your awareness of your innate nature. You may expand your view and experience your spiritual nature in whatever way you are most comfortable in defining it.

To empower your life journey, you must develop greater awareness of your true nature, the power within that is the spiritual aspect of your being. Since the primary truth and expression of man is Spirit, awareness of that aspect of self brings forth new hope, new possibilities, and unending opportunity to expand and express through that spiritual dimension. An empowered consciousness involves:

- A deepening awareness of man as a spiritual being.
- A greater capacity to experience self-love.

- Greater self-knowledge expanding into spiritual knowing.
- Viewing life's joys and challenges with equanimity.
- Maintaining this even-mindedness in changing circumstances.

False Core Ideas

The disempowered consciousness usually feels alienated from, separated from, or unable to adequately access, the Infinite Source, God or Spirit. Such thinking may take many forms:

- I am uncertain that God or a spiritual reality exists.
- The spiritual dimension is beyond my ability to know.
- My spiritual efforts feel insignificant or futile.
- I am limited in my ability to connect with the divine.
- I am unworthy to penetrate into, or to know, God.
- I have no capacity to discover spiritual Truth.
- I feel separate from the spiritual realm, whatever that is.
- I do not know how to connect with the Divine.
- I believe that life in the physical, material world is the only reality; it is pointless to focus on spirituality.
- We are only physical; nothing survives after death.
- I have insufficient faith to be "saved," a concept developed in Weber's *Protestant Ethic and Spirit of Capitalism*.
- When I am a better person, or more spiritually advanced, then I will have a relationship with God.
- I am too imperfect to offer meaningful, spiritual service. (Why would God ever want to use me to do His work?)
- I am unable, or unworthy, to view myself as a soul.
- No one can understand God, so why try?

- My faith, prayers and spiritual efforts have no real impact and serve no real purpose.

Do any of these ideas resonate with you?

Why are these Core Ideas false?

Man cannot be separate from Spirit, for man is Spirit and Spirit is constantly striving to create union, communion, and re-awakening in us. You have the power to awaken your consciousness to the truth of your deep and profound relationship with the divine source of all creation. It all begins with the *dynamic intention* to know.

The delusional idea of separation from Spirit underlies most feelings of aloneness, suffering, isolation, and desperation. All great suffering and deep anguish contains that wrong notion of man's separation from the source of all creation, his disbelief in his power as a spiritual being.

Ironically, you may feel unworthy to penetrate into that dimension even though it is the source of your own creation. As we have seen, your worthiness and deservedness are tied to the truth of your divinity and the spark of creation that resides in you. Your spiritual growth is tied to eliminating those wrong ideas of separation so you can experience more of yourself instead. That experience will increase your awareness of your connection with others and all life in the vibrational energy of love.

> *All great evil in the world springs from the delusive thought that man is separate from Spirit.*

Resistance to Deeper Spiritual Realization

Five causes usually underpin resistance to our greater spiritual realization:

1. Ignorance or confusion about how to work toward greater spiritual realization.

> *Remember, Spirit created the gift of you. You are divinity expressing itself. Remember, the world is changed because you are.*

2. Deservedness issues created by negative self-dialogue and self-talk.
3. Insufficient self-esteem to counter criticism and judgment from those who fear your efforts to journey where they have not gone.
4. Shame or guilt around entering the spiritual dimension in a different way than you were taught.
5. The nature of duality—the push-pull of positive and negative energies—which can interfere with your forward movement.

Purposeful Intention to Increase Spiritual Awareness

The foundation of love is within and accessible to all. By delving into your inner life and continuing your spiritual efforts, you can come to higher states of self-realization and even resonate with the vibrational energy of God. As you allow yourself to feel the self-love explored earlier in this chapter, your ability to love others will inevitably increase. As you connect lovingly with others and with all life, you experience the expansion of your own self-knowing. In this circular cycle, increasing any dimension of loving or awareness increases your perception of the interconnectedness of all life. Each discovery increases the capacity to discover more.

Dynamic intention is behind all accomplishments. That also includes the achievement of deeper knowing in the spiritual realm. If you wait passively and relinquish your knowing to feelings of futility, unworthiness, and lack of deservedness, you will make minimal progress in your search and the integration with your own spirituality. As noted, the idea of separation from that infinite source underlies man's experience of aloneness and desperation in his own life. "The mass of men lead lives of quiet desperation," observed Henry David Thoreau, the 19th century Transcendentalist. If you hold such a vision of disconnection, you limit your capacity to live fully.

Dynamic intention to know more must precede any genuine quest or expansion. To know more of divine energy, experiment with this idea: "What if it is possible to have a personal relationship with the Divine and thus to experience greater direct knowing?" Resolving to overcome your own resistance and that of others will create a power surge from within. That power surge will be supported by the forces of light and love.

An Invitation to Experience Direct Spiritual Knowledge

If someone does not believe in God, or a higher power, no amount of debate, or intellectual positioning, will bring them to faith. However, the ability to access the spiritual dimension resides even within those who do not believe, for that knowing is beyond intellectual ideas and is accessible regardless of your faith, your religion, or spiritual belief system. Even your feelings of worth, or feelings of unworthiness, cannot thwart the truth of your spiritual realization. It is only necessary to have a sincere desire, purposeful intention, and sufficiently powerful techniques to allow for direct experience of the Divine. Words and testimonies, spiritual works, books and ideas invite the mind and sustain inspiration for the journey to the Divine. But it is the direct experience of *touching the face of the Infinite* in whatever language or conceptualization you attach to the experience that allows you to validate and redefine your vision of yourself and of the infinite source of all knowing power.

Increasing Your Own Experience in Direct-Knowing

Key points:

- **Dynamic intention-** Formulate your desire(s) to experience more of God, or gain clarity regarding your own spiritual path.

- **Energize that dynamic intention-** Use focused will to energize intention, the arrow seeking the bull's eye of desire.

- **Petition the source –** The Eternal Source can respond immediately and directly. Ask that more will be revealed to you.

- **Affirm your spiritual expansion and awareness**. Use affirmation(s) around this powerful intention of direct experience. Example: *"I give thanks for I am in a state of direct communion and direct experience with the Divine and my own sacred nature."* Affirm it to yourself and the Divine! Energize the affirmation that has been repeated with sincerity. Continue your efforts in spite of possible feelings of unworthiness. Perseverance is key. Whatever your misgivings, always proceed as if your intention will elicit a spiritual response.

- **Practice relaxation**. Relaxation may be enhanced by placing an intention and acting as if you are relaxed. Relaxation allows for greater access to both the unconscious mind and the super-conscious energy of the Divine, whereas tension activates the restless mind and circular replay of thoughts.

- **Cultivate the habit of gratitude** as if you already had the divine response to your desire. Gratitude is a magnet for divine response. Gratitude, over time, cultivates true devotion and becomes a dynamic tool in your efforts to create deliberate happiness

- **Read inspirational and spiritual material before prayer.** If this is not a regular habit for you, begin with the goal of reading inspirational and spiritual thoughts for at least fifteen minutes a day. Also remember, thoughts planted in the consciousness prior to sleep or in deep relaxation tend to go deeper into consciousness, connecting more readily with the spiritual Source.

> *Each of us has a soul but we forget to value it. We don't remember that we are creatures made in the image of God. We don't understand the great secrets hidden inside of us.*
>
> ST. TERESA OF AVILA

- **Use prayer and affirmation.** Use the prayer techniques that you find most comfortable remembering that even if you do not believe in a spiritual aspect of life, proceed as if it exists. By grace, you can experience divine awakening, divine realization, and penetrate into the power of love and light. The divine interconnectedness of all life will be revealed to you.

- **Experience peace in silence.** Know that devotion grows in silence and cultivate a peaceful consciousness. **Affirmations** related to peace and quality **meditation** techniques into your daily life will enhance this experience. Silence allows for a deeper dive into the sacred waters of spirit.

Why Make Spiritual Effort?

If you are content, feel peace, joy, and a direct experience of unconditional love, there may be no need to proceed further. If, however, like most people, you desire to experience more peace, more inner fulfillment, more joy, and greater access to divine love, then more effort will be well worth it. Continue to break down your efforts in small steps, and be consistent so that you develop the habit of spiritual striving. Too many giant steps may result in discouragement about reaching a new level of self-embrace and knowledge of your spiritual nature.

How Self Love Can Lead to Change and Empowerment

If you believe a circumstance or situation cannot be changed, your will to change stagnates. While not all situations and circumstances can be changed completely, some aspects can change, improvements can be made and greater acceptance achieved. As we have seen before, reframing and other techniques give us immense power to transform thoughts and consciousness and from this new power to create deliberate happiness.

The Serenity Prayer as a Guidepost for Living

The Serenity Prayer embodies a living philosophy for the empowerment of life. By using this simple prayer as a guidepost, you can incorporate practical wisdom that can transform your life, bringing balance, grace and acceptance. The key is to increase discernment and discrimination, to accept life as it comes, change what you can, and leave the rest in the hands of a Higher Power. Making this prayer a part of daily life can support you in good times and difficult ones.

Learning to say the serenity prayer on a regular basis, and developing a philosophy of living around its principles, can reveal when to forge ahead and when to surrender. But how do we discern what conditions are beyond altering? Sometimes your best efforts cannot impact the unmovable. In such challenges, you should attempt to identify the areas that you can change. Not only should you attempt to identify them, but you should journal about them as a way of clarifying and focusing instead of merely reacting emotionally.

Going Deeper: Name the problem. Examine solutions

When confronting a problem, difficulty, or obstacle, focus on objectively naming it and then assessing solutions.

1. <u>Gain Clarity</u>: You cannot change what you don't see or understand. Identifying the problem, or blockage, is the first step. Name it. Label it. Attempt to analyze your feelings of vulnerability around this problem. Is there fear? Has the problem already occurred, or do you believe it will occur? Do you believe that God, or the universe, will provide for you? Is your effort required?

   > *God grant me the serenity to accept the things I cannot change; courage to change the things I can; and wisdom to know the difference.*
   >
   > REINHOLD NIEBUHR
   > *Stepping Stones to Recovery, as quoted by Bill Pittman*

2. <u>Evaluate solutions</u>: A helpful way of approaching solutions is to brainstorm all possible solutions, both practical and impractical. Use your imagination. Be creative. This will diminish any fear that is present and begin a more creative process.

3. <u>Small Steps</u>: After creating your list of solutions, write down a number of small steps that you can take that may positively impact your difficulties in some manner. Write down what attitudes you could change. Perhaps a calm discussion with someone involved will create a better climate for understanding or collaboration.

4. <u>Find the Origin</u>: Before determining what can or cannot be changed, establish where the problem originates. Did it come from your own thoughts, words or behavior? Or were conditions created by some outside source? Identify whether

the problem is actually your problem or whether it belongs to someone else. Ask "Whose problem is this anyway?" Then ask other related questions: "Who has the power to change?" and "Who needs to change?"

5. <u>Let Go</u>: Be willing to release and give back the problems which are not yours. This act of discernment and release can save us much grief, feelings of futility, and hopelessness. We all have enough of our own problems without borrowing the real or imagined problems of others. Analyze if you are spending a great deal of worry and energy around the need for someone else to make changes.

Will God Help in Your Difficulty Achieving Empowerment?

Feelings of stagnation and futility are fueled by the circular emotions of hopelessness and despair. Few things are so powerful in their impact upon us as these feelings. They also create a sense of aloneness, isolation, separation from others and from the Divine Source. You can move from hopelessness and despair by beginning to claim the power within, even in small ways at first. Viewing yourself as a dynamic creator you can uproot some feelings of hopelessness and impotency. Assessing and re-evaluating your spirituality also empowers.

God has ever been with you and will always be there for you; your inability to acknowledge the presence of God does not determine whether or not God exists. Too often we may believe that God must change the world according to our conceptions or perceptions, in order for us to believe in His existence. Either God exists, or God does not exist. Our beliefs—your belief system— does not matter.

God is powerfully present; there is no life beyond the scope and power of that Divine Love. Personal empowerment is challenging without some relationship with a Higher Power or idea of the

Divine. A life without a spiritual foundation may be meaningful and satisfying, but no matter how you live your life, the truth of your mortality, is inescapable.

Another common feeling during times of hardship is that the Divine will rescue us. Perhaps what needs to be remedied is our consciousness. We need to clarify whether we first can act to change our circumstances. As we have seen some conditions are intractable and cannot be changed, but many can be affected by our attitudes and actions. Do you believe that by passively wishing for God to bring a job, a mate, or other desires, those things will materialize?

The great Indian Seer, Paramahansa Yogananda, used to often say: "God helps those who help themselves." You need to become aware of times when you passively wish your circumstances to change and when you exercise your own imagination and intention. Are you following up with our own will-directed activity? If you desire God to help you find the right career or job, then you also need to examine practical steps to get there. While waiting for God to deliver that job to your door, are you applying for jobs? Are you contacting people who may help? Are you networking? Or do you expect that God will find a way to provide for you without your participating in your own volitional activities? None of us is exempt from confronting the fragile, vulnerable parts of ourselves. The only way the vulnerable parts can be confronted is with the arms of love and the tenderness of patience.

LIFE IS A SCHOOL

You can experience life as a training ground for greater self-awareness, self-growth, self-knowing, self-loving—all the aspects of personal empowerment. This metaphysical perspective includes an inherent assumption that there is a positive payoff and benefit to every experience and every challenge that you face.

Underlying this belief is the attitude that life is a school and that this school is designed with great and ample opportunity to learn and grow. We are all in different classrooms, according to our specific needs. Some may face growth challenges as they confront health issues; others may focus on relationships. As we internalize these growth lessons that can expand us, we move on. We "graduate" to new lessons. As we increase our self-knowledge, we become more aware of who we are. *This is the ultimate sacred invitation – to become awake in self-knowing.* True self-knowing is Self-realization in which we penetrate the divine aspect.

Empowerment requires that you recognize and respond to both highly positive, affirming experiences and negative, challenging ones. To see events and conditions in your life as sacred invitations involves a major paradigm shift, THE paradigm shift which encompasses a new and profound metaphysical understanding of how you create meaning in your life. The challenges with which you are presented are not random, nor without higher purpose. All can offer opportunities for growth. This shift involves believing that the laws of the universe are not random and chaotic, but instead operate according to spiritual law.

Ordinarily we do not see the interconnectedness of flowing events in our lives, so we may feel that things happen to us randomly. Thus you may also fall into victim consciousness, unaware that spiritual laws are in operation, impacting your life. How you live consciously in the Now creates energy flows, which will then create your future. Your tenacious mental habits generate new energy flows that operate according to spiritual law. Events you experience arise out of your own consciousness, as well as your actions. Because thoughts,

> *Our life journey is not just the journey of luck or chance. It is about the powerful movement of evolving energies that are more than the sum total of any singular event.*

actions and behaviors of an earlier time may take months or even years to manifest, you may not be aware of the "cause and effect" relationship.

As these truths about the operation of spiritual law incubate and as you begin to embody them more and more, you grow in understanding, wisdom, and alignment with the Divine. Your decision to explore and attempt to create harmony between the two energies of the Limited and Eternal Selves is a step toward true personal empowerment and deliberate happiness. Conversely all acts of personal growth and empowerment contribute to bringing the Limited Self into a full union with the Eternal Self.

Reframing Your Experiences

Reframing is an important practical tool, especially in the context of your personal empowerment.

- Reframing moves you out of victim consciousness toward accessing your power, including the power to change.
- Reframing inspires you to see life's challenges as learning opportunities and thus, to develop the habit of gratitude.

As you continue to develop the ability to reframe events and circumstances in the most positive light, you begin to recognize that "all things work together for good" to those who love, respect and honor universal principles. You begin to see that there is a divine rhythm and pattern to life--an underlying oneness in all created things. This sense of unity in all life, the awareness that you live, move and have your being in the Universal dance, provides the security, peace and well-being from which true empowerment can spring.

> *Spiritual law exists and connects events both seen and unseen.*

Cultivating an Empowered Attitude

These paradigm shifts in consciousness entail seeing experiences as more than just coincidence. You cannot penetrate the movement of universal and spiritual forces by your cognitive faculties alone. Energy operates according to greater cosmic laws than you may ever fully grasp with the intellect. But they move precisely according to a higher spiritual law.

Accepting these laws is critical to leading an empowered life. How can you develop such an approach?

1. By moving from a psychological paradigm to a metaphysical paradigm in your perspective.
2. By accepting that life is a spiritual journey and not just a biological and psychological one.
3. By cultivating the perspective that whatever has occurred has had a higher purpose for the greater good.
4. By renaming and reframing: As you rename, you will claim.
5. By appreciating the opportunity for transformation inherent in experience.
6. By embracing opportunities for growth and change.
7. By limiting the time you spend in the past and in the future, thus perfecting living in the Now.

These steps will assist you in broadening your perspective and accepting that your life is the unfolding of both your actions and your attitudes. The unfolding is activated through the flow of energy and the blueprints in the ether. These blueprints were preliminarily shaped by the past, but become energized by our present habits in consciousness.

The challenge, then, is this: How do we define the events that have been set in motion? Are they the result of unseen or unknown energies in the universe? Or are the events created by insufficient attention to our behavior and our choices? Too often we blame fate for that which we create ourselves.

Some events already in motion will not be altered by any level of insight, action, or effort to change. Then there are events that can be dramatically altered by an increase in self-understanding, self-knowledge, and candor. The less defensive you are, the more you will be open to learning the lessons life brings through circumstances and relationships. That is why you must explore yourself with even-mindedness, knowing that this will ultimately empower you. Your goal is not self-blame, but rather self-knowledge as a prelude to self-empowerment.

> *Our thoughts literally draw real and solid 'things' from the multiple possibilities involved in our entire existence. Quantum scientists are now conducting measurable experiments, never before thought possible, to prove the theory - **consciousness creates reality.***
>
> MELANIE TONIA EVANS

Changing Your Perspective, You Empower Change in Reality

Are you waiting to be happy when problems cease? You need to release the fallacy that one day all problems will end. A true accomplishment in life is learning to be happy when problems intensify! As long as you are in a physical body, in a material world, you will never see the end of difficulties. Since that is the case, you must not equate happiness with the end of problems or difficulties. Instead, you need to shift your view of what will give you happiness.

Personal growth comes from meeting and confronting life's challenges as invitations, for your problems are tied, in some manner, to your past or present consciousness. You need to exert your power to see, change, and act by taking charge of your consciousness and its impact on your activities.

Cultivating Awareness of the Divine

True personal empowerment lies in deepening your awareness of your connection with Spirit. Whether you entertain the idea of God in a formalized aspect, or as a force or power in the universe, you are acknowledging a source higher than yourself. By entertaining the possibility of something bigger than yourself, you naturally move into direct connection with that larger presence. If you believe that a Higher Source is separate from you, you will limit your experience accordingly. True empowerment requires opening to your spiritual dimension and the truth that you are inseparably connected with the Source that created you. Nothing you ever think, do or say can alter that reality. No matter how dark the path may be at times, this message provides a lantern of hope to guide you on your way.

Cultivating the Authentic Voice

Cultivating an authentic voice is an important part of your spiritual quest. Your authentic voice is the sound of spirit in vocalized words speaking with the authority of Truth. An authentic voice is vibrationally aligned with truth and expresses the intonation of that truth through the Eternal Self.

Remember, the two selves are frequently in a place of disharmony. The Limited Self is based on ego-identification with the body and the physical world. If that Limited Self is to speak your "truth" it is expressing the multi-layered aspects of personality, perception, and life experiences that are self-based and world-based. Many people believe that to speak one's truth is to verbalize any opinion or emotion. Opinions are opinions and emotions are emotions! Not all are of equal value and some may not be in spiritual alignment with truth. Standing in one's truth does not mean venting every emotion, memory or wound. Discharging what is in your ego-based personality is not speaking from a place of truth, rather it is speaking from a place of ego-based perception.

The Limited Self may claim an authentic voice, but its perspective is not broad enough to incorporate the idea and truth inherent in the Eternal Self. An authentic voice is pure, uncontaminated by ego, emotions, or agendas that are related to personality. Speaking your truth can be a weapon of assault and attack, if that "truth" is spoken from the perspective of the Limited Self. Real truth has nothing to do with your ego-based consciousness operating through the Limited Self. Speaking your truth has real power when aligned with the higher Self. Then you engage, not with the ego, but with the soul of another. Truth is partial when seen through the eyes of the Limited Self, absolute when expressed through the eyes of the Eternal Self.

Many therapists encourage speaking up, speaking out, releasing repressed material. The benefits of confronting suppressed or repressed material and confronting fears are real and often healing. However, creating a bridge between the Limited and the Eternal Self is seldom a priority in psychotherapy. Many approaches to therapy tie to a better integration of the Limited Self with itself, and preclude the idea of aligning two diverging selves.

When people encourage others to speak their truth, often what they mean is that the individual needs to speak up. The question is then, "speak up from where?" From what perspective, from what experience, and from what part of the personality or the self are you speaking? Speaking up, or speaking one's truth, often means giving people permission to vent. And venting is tied almost entirely to perceptions, feelings, and ideas of the Limited Self. On the other hand, truth with a capital "T" is tied to the Eternal Self. With the Limited Self, as ideas and perceptions change the subjects of those perceptions and ideas will change too, for ideas move and grow and we internalize new ones. Truth with a capital "T" is unchanging for it resonates with Spirit.

When the Eternal Self speaks truth, you express yourself through your authentic voice. Authenticity resonates with Spirit. It is Spirit in expression, resonating with pure spiritual power, strength, and vibrancy. When truth and sound align, spiritual power is unlocked and vibrates. As you work on a greater alignment between the Limited Self and the Eternal Self, your words become charged with greater power to manifest, for the authentic voice is God speaking. Many times individuals who have been in circumstances of parental disconnection or abuse find that their power to speak genuinely, from the heart, has been compromised. Greater empowerment does not mean turning up the volume of one's voice, but renewed effort in claiming the core of oneself. In that core resides peace and reverence for life. When you access that core, you find your connection to all life and humanity, including yourself.

Speaking one's truth is about the resonance of love, the resonance of self-appreciation. It is about valuing life, about the reflection of Divine Light in the powerful vibratory energy of sound. It is about the Divine within us expressing with increasing power. Key ideas:

- Often in childhood, for whatever reason, the child doubts the value of his/her own voice. Authoritarian approaches that assume children should be seen and not heard, squelch the child's sense of personal value and/or their worth. Consistent dysfunctional interactions between parents and children also result in a diminished sense of self that minimizes the importance of the child's own voice. You are a unique and powerful spiritual magnet that can resonate with Spirit when your authentic voice expresses your spiritual alignment with self.

- Speaking up indiscriminately is not exercising your authentic voice. Nor does the authentic voice cut off the power of another's voice. The authentic voice graciously invites ideas and exchanges with others in respectful dialogue.

- It is never too late to cultivate a powerful, authentic voice. Begin by affirming the light and the power of the divine essence within, while honoring the divinity within the soul of another.

- One technique for cultivating an authentic voice is to increase the "I AM" statements that reflect divine truth. Another involves repeating spiritual ideas in affirmative formats. Such statements recognize the divinity of God that is expressing in each and every individual interacting with you.

- Affirmations: "The divinity of God is manifesting within each and every soul that I am experiencing." And, "My capacity to discern the divinity of God in every soul daily is increasing." These affirmations can be done individually or together.

When you perceive that another has taken your power, you respond defensively. Often you may feel the need to attack, belittle, or criticize another in response. But no other person has the ability to take away your power. When you perceive your power has been taken from you that is usually because your Limited Self is insufficiently integrated with the Eternal Self. You perceive from the ego-based personality of the Limited Self whereas, if you have aligned the two selves, you will be able to respond from your center of self-knowing, to feel that power of self-knowledge and self-integration. Perhaps you did not understand that center was available to you. There may be times when you do not take a stand because you either do not perceive that you have the choice, or you do not know how to exercise that choice. But peace at any cost is not peace, especially if the cost is relinquishing your true self.

The authentic voice speaks from its own base of power, taking ownership of the "I" statements about itself. You state how things impact you, or how you perceive, owning your experiences without the need to assault others. You have the capacity to speak in your authentic voice. The power is within; exercising it will empower you.

You are an Extraordinary Bearer of Gifts

The world is brighter because you are here; vow to increase your light by delivering even more gifts. The greatest gift is who you are, but sometimes we do not see that sparkling light because a small voice sends loud resounding messages that "you aren't good enough." Affirm your value and become even more valuable.

Key ideas in empowering yourself to create deliberate happiness:

- Be fully present in the Now. You cannot co-exist in both the Now and in the future.

- Learn the lessons from the past. Do not become a prisoner of what has already happened to you.

- Assess your engagement in the present moment and how it may impact the future.

- The art of communicating is first to hear, not speak. The solution for another may be the gift of feeling truly heard by you. Give the gift of listening, not problem-solving. Reflect back what you believe the other person is attempting to communicate. Often we fail to hear because we so desire to be part of the solution.

- The gift of being fully present with another human being is giving the gift of the four "C's: caring, communication, connection, and compassion. These four "C's" are vital gifts needed by every human being. You may increase that energy by giving the gift of time, mentoring, teaching, or example.

Spiritual Service

All great spiritual literature testifies to the many ways in which the universe makes highly imperfect human beings the means to extraordinary ends. You may already see how many of the "imperfect" people around you serve to better the world and the lot of their fellow men. You do not become a better spiritual instrument by waiting to become perfect. It is in giving, with genuineness of intention and the desire for service, that you will become more of who you are. So place your intention on becoming more attuned to Spirit. Affirm that intention and make some concrete effort at giving more or serving more, with sincere intent.

Spiritual service is also a pathway to loving yourself more as well as providing powerful remedies for deservedness issues. The idea that you become worthy by waiting until you feel worthy will limit you to a passive life. As we have seen, deservedness issues can cloud your perception of who you are and trap you in inadequate psychological paradigms. Your inability to directly perceive who you truly are creates further feelings of inadequacy and unworthiness. In reviewing the lives of those who serve, try to identify how many were perfect people? Great and wondrous things have and will continue to manifest through imperfect people.

The irony is that you may be hesitant to hear the call of action until you are certain God is calling you, or that you are worthy to be called. Your first breath as a living, loving being filled with the energy of God was the first trumpet call to love and to give service. Heighten your discrimination. Strive for attunement to the higher good and to the higher source.

Remember this: there is much work to be done on the earth and a shortage of perfect people to do it. Therefore, God must be content with the work of imperfect people. Strive to become more perfected by continuing to go forward with perseverance even in the most discouraging times and conditions. If you think of yourself as a divine instrument of the good, you give yourself permission to expand all the ways in which you might serve. Always strive for attunement with that higher power! Be vigorous in your efforts of introspection and self-dialogue! Be willing to change course, or direction, if need be. Do not become too attached to what the pathway must look like. Keep your focus on the goal or destination.

Hear the Voice of The Other

Empowerment in hearing others also means expanding the art of hearing yourself and attending to the repetition of themes in self-talk. As we have discussed in earlier chapters, honest self-dialogue is necessary in developing the art of hearing yourself. Give yourself permission to explore yourself so that you might hear another. If you don't cultivate sufficient self-understanding and self-knowledge, there is the danger that you will find yourself compromised in your ability to hear other people. The problem may be that you begin to project your own themes onto another and believe that the projection is what another is saying. Self-dialogue is a tool that allows you to understand yourself and the other.

> *We are what we think. All that we are arises with our thoughts. With our thoughts we make our world.*
>
> GAUTAMA BUDDHA

Hearing the voice of the other is more than the art of listening. Hearing the voice of another involves participating in all aspects of yourself. It also involves communion and communication with the higher spiritual aspects of another. It is another level of spiritual alignment and recognition of the soul essence of yourself and the other. When you are present in the Now, you participate more in the Eternal Self and less in the Limited Self. And when you hear the voice of the other, you expand the spiritual empowerment of yourself and of that other person.

Increase Your Awareness and Your Attention to Other People as a Path to Spiritual Empowerment

Focus on what you can change within yourself. Emphasize being more fully present. Emphasize listening with greater attentiveness without diluting your focus by trying to find solutions. The solution, first and foremost, is to hear.

> *Emotional intimacy is increased by increasing your ability to hear other people.*

You cannot change another's capacity. You can, however, reinforce their positive efforts in connecting, communicating, or being present with you. Learn to praise sincerely the efforts of others and you will shape their behavior to increasingly make more effort in the areas you are encouraging. Do not dilute your positive recognition of another by negative statements. Positive reinforcement never suggests "yes, but" as you give sincere recognition. Your "yeses" and praise should not be qualified by statements that take away from the initial intention. Be willing to enter into dialogue where you do not feel compelled to supply all the answers.

Emotional intimacy involves listening. All of us desire that someone else might truly know us, see us, hear us, and love us. That desire to feel a powerful connection with another person, or others, appears to be universal. True emotional intimacy involves the willingness to take time to hear what is being said, as well as attending to that which is being left unsaid. Hearing is not only listening with the ears, but with the heart.

Listening with the heart is a direct expression of empathy. Empathy is the capacity of the heart to interact with the heart of another. This requires a shifting of attention

> *All things are our relatives; what we do to everything, we do to ourselves. All is really One.*
> — BLACK ELK

from yourself, and your ego-based consciousness, to another person. The act of shifting your attention outside of your physical, ego-based consciousness actually allows a greater shift, a movement toward the Eternal Self. That shift occurs when you relinquish energy that is strongly tied to your identification with the Limited Self. That energy moves towards its center in the core of the Higher Self.

Become a Communicator

Communication involves more than words. Communication occurs at multiple wordless levels by inflection, bodily expression, gesture and projection of feeling states. What is being said is never just the sum total of words.

As you become more centered in the quiet of yourself, you will generously expand your true ability to hear. Hearing others is a function of the ears and the heart. It begins with the art of being present in the moment, being present in the Now. Listening to what someone says is the first step. Reflective listening in which you clarify your understanding of what you heard comes next. This understanding will result in greater emotional intimacy and deeper friendships.

An Invitation to the Sacred Walk

The spiritual dimension resides within and is accessible to you regardless of your Faith, your religion, your spiritual beliefs, your feelings of worth, or feelings of unworthiness. Words and testimonies, spiritual works, books and ideas invite the mind to journey toward the direct experience of *touching the face of the Infinite* in whatever conceptualization we attach to that experience. That experience becomes an invitation to the sacred walk.

I Walked the Roads of Earth

*I walked the roads of earth
And combed the lands.
I listened to the call of life
And answered the voice of man.*

*I walked the roads of earth
Till my soul did soar on high
And come to rest,
The timeless rest
There on forms of light.
I nestled in Nirvana's nest
Where I knew the soundless sounds
And nourished on the airless breath.
There I knew birth
And vanquished death.*

*And there ever have I been
And yet again, I've left
There beyond the calling.
Desire called to me
And I longed to feel the weight of flesh
And hear the songs of man.
I longed to see the timeless march
And watch the drifting sand.*

*So once again I walk the roads of earth:
The ray of light has made the matter journey.*

Life is a dualistic play of light and dark. Your movement toward accessing more light stirs the opposing polarity of energy, for the world is not simply a playground of the light and of positive forces. The power of resistance is the pull of the negative to which you should never submit, but rather continue forward affirming your protection in the light, affirming the divine protection of yourself. Be aware that the whispers of your own self-doubts are the whispers of the negative force of the universe. Remember, the negative whispers do not have a greater reality than the truth of your divine nature. You are strongly connected to the infinite light and that infinite reality. This is one reason why affirmations are such a powerful tool when you are assaulted by your own negative self-dialogue. You always have the ability to change that negativity to spiritual connection and knowledge directly received from the God force. You always can stand firm in your personal and spiritual empowerment.

Potent Power Thoughts

1. **Empowered people are present in the Now.** The past is the past and the morrows may never be. We only have this moment in time. Cease splitting time and giving it to the past and to the future. Be present in this moment in time. Your power is in the Now.

2. **Discover your inner treasure by meditation, the true power source.** In the Now, vow to journey within. You have the power to master meditation, a path of interiorized consciousness. Discover this inner treasure, for you are the treasure you are seeking.

3. **Fuel your renewed effort with dynamic intention and will to become increasingly empowered.** Dynamic will can become the dynamo driving your power to create. Resolve to make the effort. Place your intention, and your internal dynamo will alter the unfolding possibilities. Greater empowerment will be yours.

4. **Create and strengthen positive habits in consciousness.** Strengthen your positive habits in consciousness while weakening and eradicating any negative habitual thoughts by energized affirmations, statements that affirm the good. Your habits in consciousness may be the mine field (or mind field!) between you and your happiness and joy. Your inner power may be hidden by the shadows of those negative habits in consciousness. You are powerful enough to create new habits just as you made the old. Those new habits can unlock the power of the sun and the shining presence of yourself. Affirm and meditate!

5. **Create a gratitude/thankfulness journal.** Write in this journal to express a positive thought, experience, memory or reflection. State: I am grateful that life is providing me the opportunity

    - to learn,
    - to experience,
    - to awaken.

    I value this moment in time to reflect on life's gifts, on my knowing, on my doing, on my being.

6. **Explore the Self:** Become an adventurer and courageous explorer of the vast recesses of the self by

    - meditating,
    - affirming your power in spirit-centered affirmations,
    - journaling,
    - introspection,
    - engaging in self-dialogue and self-discovery,
    - welcoming assistance from qualified fellow travelers or competent professionals, and
    - emulating spiritual messengers who validate the law of love and unselfish service.

7. **Become the Author of Your Own Life Play:** You are the writer, the author, the artist. Use the medium of framing and reframing to redefine meaning and to bring texture, color and radiance to your journey. Become the hero of your own story, and not the victim of changing circumstances. Your creative power is innate. You are the artistic master creating within yourself.

8. **Demolish Deservedness Issues:** Freedom awaits and your life can become power-charged when you break through the chains of deservedness issues. Those issues had their origin in some form of neglect, disconnected parenting, abuse or severe lack. Their origin was in early trauma and your mind's interpretation of those events. The same power of the mind to interpret can be unlocked to re-interpret, to create, to visualize and re-visualize new, energized possibilities for yourself. Those can include stoking the flame of your own creativity to bring greater abundance into your life. Remember you can affirm, frame and re-frame your story.

> Magnetic creator of possibilities,
> Meditate into the chambers of your potency.
> Affirm the truth of your being, Magnetic creator
> Your power is in Knowing.

9. **Name Your Themes:** Identify a core obstacle to your power and happiness. Identify and uproot two core deservedness issues. What do you say to yourself when a serious upheaval erupts in your life? What are your themes? Here are some common examples:

    - I am unloved.
    - I am a failure.
    - Everything I try fails.
    - I'll never amount to anything.
    - I'm worthless, etc. etc. etc.

Once you have defined these themes, use spiritualized affirmations to confront your feelings of unworthiness. You might repeat, "I am a divine child of God (or "of the universe," or whatever words you use to describe your higher power). Another affirmation is "I am powerful in co-creation with the universe. All successes are powerfully manifesting Now!"

10. **Expand Your Authenticity.** Like more. Praise more. Thank more. Love more. By shifting your consciousness to such attitudes you train your mind to create a reservoir of the positive within. You move from a puddle jumper of shifting likes and dislikes to being a navigator of vaster seas. These steps better integrate the Limited and Eternal Self. With that, your capacity to express your true, authentic Self majestically presents itself. Greater integration of the two Selves allows you to express the centered self authentically, and the world around you becomes changed by your expression of powerful, new positive energy.

11. **Deepen and expand your meaningful relationships with others.** Become a better friend, neighbor or mentor by improving your listening skill and practicing hearing instead of solving. You could make a list of small gestures, acts that you know could help someone out. Survey your talents and the skills that you can contribute or teach. Believe in one child, and also extend your effort as a coach, teacher, helper, mentor or friend. As you celebrate yourself and celebrate others, erase gossip. Thoughts and talk about the personal business of others dams up your personal power and joy. Focus instead on the power of your consciousness and the potency of your kindness.

12. **Claim your power as a co-creator with the Divine.** Your creativity is without limit. It exists within you, and without in the vast reservoir of creation itself, the mother and father of creativity. Repeat the affirmation: The divine creativity is within me.

I am manifesting it as a co-creator with the Divine." Balanced meditation techniques are the pathway toward a stronger union with your higher self. Patience and perseverance allow the creative to fully manifest. Know you are ever creating and expanding creation itself!

13. **Expand both your imagination and your heart.** Plant a garden of possibilities in your imagination and your heart. Your imagination is the light that sketches your image making in creation. Your heart is the light of love pulsating from the source of all. Cultivate both imagination and heart with spiritualized affirmations, meditation and practicing gratitude. Your image making can create universes of possibilities. Your heart can expand the world itself.

14. **Accept Sacred Invitations.** Embark on your life anew as if called by a sacred invitation. Life itself is a sacred invitation presenting circumstances we meet or create that are the perfect divine vehicle to discover the self and the Divine. All things manifesting are sacred invitations to self-discovery. View your experiences as sacred invitations for expansion, self-knowledge and empowerment in actualized knowing.

15. **Believe in Miracles—and if you don't, act as if you do!** The universe operates according to physical and spiritual laws—both seen and unseen. Universal laws do not govern you because of your beliefs. Proceed *as if* you believe that miraculous intercession is possible in all things. Your shift in consciousness to entertaining the idea of miracles is sufficient enough to open the doors of attuned magnetism and the laws of attraction. The unexplainable can manifest! There is another important universal law, the law of grace. It supersedes the laws of cause and effect, for it moves with the power of love, the foundation of all in the universe. Believe in miracles. You are one yourself.

Powerful, Miraculous You

*Powerful, miraculous you,
worthy essence of light,
claim your due.
You deserve to claim the All,
The All itself bows to you.*

*You are condensed starlight,
Divine sparks and emanations,
congealed into miraculous you.
God's vision took form
in the magnificence of who you are.
Your existence calls the stars
to shine even brighter.
With your words the I am
is summoned.
With your prayers the moon
softens the night
and the sun illumines a brighter day.
You have awakened them
by your power to know
and because you are.*

*Powerful, miraculous you,
worthy essence of light,
claim your due.
You deserve to claim the All,
The All itself bows to you.*

Affirmations for Empowerment

To Awaken Initiative
Awaken Volcanic Power
of initiative.
Soaring energy
of force and radiance,
I claim Thee.
Awaken Volcanic Power
of initiative.
(note: the last two lines of this affirmation can be used as a stand alone.)

For More Light
I am powerful
for I am Spirit
encased in light.
I emanate that light.
I am that light.

For Grateful Claiming
With gratitude
I claim
the inward
splendor.
With gratitude
I claim
the infinite
bliss.

For Expressing Truth and Knowing
I am aligned with truth.
I express divine truth.
The truth of love manifests from me.
The truth of love manifests from God. I am aligned with Truth. I sit on the seat of knowing.
I am one with my highest nature.
I am awake in my knowing.

For Greater God-Realization
I am divinity
encased in form
on a journey
of self-knowing
and greater
God realization.

For the Divine Dance
The celestial music plays.
Angels dance.
Joyous is my participation.
I dance and glide
in the NOW
of omnipresence.

For Realizing My Limitless Potential.
I am a star gazer,
a star traveler.
I move in infinity
and limitless space.
I claim the infinite.
I claim the reality
of myself soaring
in all dimensions.
I am limitless potential.

For Merging into a Sea of Bliss
I am merging
into the infinite.
The boundaries of myself
dissolve
in a sea of bliss.

For Becoming One with the Power of Creation
I am one with the power
of all light, love, and all creation.
I drink from the waters of peace.
In that peace, I know that I am.
For I am one with the power
of all light, love, and all creation.

For Perfect Alignment with Myself
I am one with the universe.
I am one with myself.
In perfected alignment
I experience myself.

For Pure Being in God
I am that I am.
I am awake in God.
I am that I am.
I am that I am.
I am that I am.

For Direct Communion with the Divine
I give thanks
for I am in a state of direct
communion and direct experience
with the Divine
and my own sacred nature.

For Claiming My Light
Claim the light of yourself,
for you are the captured light of the sun.
I am the captured light of the sun
and the brilliant emanations
of the stars in the night.
I am the breath of God breathing
for a higher purpose.

For Creating Stars and Universes
I am divinity encased,
starlight contained.
I move as a force,
creating worlds and universes
by thought bubbles of possibilities.

For Realizing My Essence, Manifesting My Truth
I am the essence of Light, itself.
I am the embodiment of power.
I am the force of all creation
hiding in flesh,
but manifesting the truth
that I am the light, the power, and the vision
that is co-creating with God.

For Knowing My Light Nature
I am the captured light of the sun
and the brilliant emanations
of the stars in the night.
I am the essence of all creation
experiencing in embodied form.

For Becoming One with the Sea of All
I am uncontained,
And I am uncontainable.
I am one with the sea of all.

For Breathing with the Spiritual Great Ones
I breathe the
breath of the
Living Christ.
The breath of
Christ and I
are one.
(The name of any spiritual deity or figure may be substituted, if desired. This is a powerful affirmation that has the ability to create higher states of divine awareness and greater attunement to the Divine.)

For Union with the Sea of Consciousness
I drink from the vast oceanic consciousness.
I sip the waters of my essence.
I merge into the sea of bliss.

For Becoming a Channel of Light and Love
My prayer is to be
a channel
of infinite light
and infinite love,
attuned to
the Divine Will.

For Coming Home Through Om
Oh Sacred Om,
call me home.
Rushing waters,
thundering sounds,
Oh Sacred Om,
call me home.
I gaze in reflective waters.
I see the peace within myself
moving as ripples
on the pond.

For Seeing My Light Moving Toward the Sea
I gaze in reflective waters.
I see the profoundness of myself.
The divinity within casts itself
as light prisms
moving toward
the waters of the sea.

For Residing in The Sanctuary of Peace
O Spirit,
The sanctuary of peace
is mine.
I am resident in quiet,
enveloping peace.
Serenity is mine
NOW.

For Penetrating Sky and Sea
One-pointed focus,
arrow like,
I penetrate the star.
I dive through
the sea of blue
and touch the golden
rim of sun.

For Goal-pointed Direction
One-pointed focus,
bow me to the goal.
Liberated self,
I penetrate the infinite.

For Penetration by Luminous Truth
Opulent pearls of wisdom
reflect Thy knowing
through me,
within me.
Luminous Truth,
penetrate me.

For Renewal of hope
Dawning hope
seize the sun
of possibilities.
The day is created
and I am born
of the dawning sun.

For Becoming Starlight
I am condensed starlight
finding my way home.
I ride the rim of gold
to that iridescent field of blue.
At the eye's center
I enter the star.
I become the star.
I become one with God.

For Finding Serenity
Still waters
Reflect Thy peace.
I am the waters
purified.
I am the light
reflecting.
I penetrate the stillness.
I am perfected in the peace.
I radiate the light.

For Light to Dispel the Darkness
Shadow specters disappear.
The light of sun has come.
I am filled with surging light
and radiant ripples in my spine,
for Thou art mine.

For Becoming Centered as a Divine Child of God
I am a Divine child of God.
My consciousness centers
And interiorizes in direct knowing.
I expand into Love waves and bliss bubbles.
I am awakening to the truth.
I am a divine child of God.

By Jacqui Freedman

CHAPTER FOUR

Epilogue

As you have seen in these chapters on empowerment, to achieve deliberate happiness you must gain understanding of your own true nature and your habits in consciousness because those habits directly determine your capacity to have relationships and to experience joy. When you increase your ability to embrace life, and all experiences are viewed as invitations to expansion and self-knowledge, you create new levels of meaning and empowerment to create deliberate happiness. This requires that you increase the flow of Spirit in your life by acknowledging your own inherent spiritual nature. The Spirit within you flows with the spiritual essence outside of yourself. The power of energized choice, imagination and vision can only be strengthened by contemplating and reflecting that the power of ALL resides in the powerhouse of consciousness within you. Perceiving these truths every moment, living in the Now and practicing their application makes you able to hear others and grow yourself. And growing, you can experience your own spiritual power.

I intend this book as a call to you to proceed along the pathway of joy itself by empowering yourself to claim more of your infinite nature. From that human, seemingly innate desire for happiness, you still sense the "more." You sense and know, at some deep level, that you are more than others know. And you are more than even you know!

My intention throughout has been to describe both practical techniques and sacred invitations to encourage traveling to these new possibilities. It is difficult to claim change and create real transformation without developing some greater understandings of your consciousness. Also, you need to build new habits and positive pathways to change. These new habits, systematically practiced, create further positive changes in consciousness and new biochemical pathways in the physical brain itself.

You possess the power of choice, change and the potential of even further empowerment. In spite of that truth, expect and anticipate that resistance will accompany your efforts to change and to establish new habits in consciousness. It is your own dissenting inner voice that you must confront. It whispers, "Who are you to believe you can?" This is the voice of duality in motion. It is the voice of the Limited Self, gripped by fear. It fears above all its own extinction and attempts to dull the voice of the higher Self calling us to self-claiming and remembrance.

Strange as it may seem, we all do encounter underlying emotional resistance to making changes that empower our lives and increase our capacity to create happiness. As we have seen, resistance originates from the Limited Self that is always fearful that change may diminish us and our powers. Yet change may actually be the bridge over which you move closer to and more empowered to experience the Eternal Self.

Not knowing how change is going to present itself contributes to inner resistance. That does not mean that you cannot make those changes. Resistance is fear-based but that does not mean you are incapable of change. It only means there is some level of uncertainty or anxiety holding you back. With divine help, you can move through fear to claim new domains in consciousness and courage.

Once you cross the bridge of change, you may come to realize that you have been carrying the dead weight of old continents on your back. You have been going forward with pieces of a world you don't need to carry instead of moving forward to new beginnings in new lands.

By viewing life as a sacred journey offering many challenges, you accept your potential to achieve greater self-knowledge and to activate greater self-awareness, while cultivating gratitude and appreciation for the good in your life. You cannot hold onto extremes in negativity and also see the positive potential ahead. The darkness of negativity obscures your own light.

If you learn to reframe your experiences around the idea of sacred invitations, you will re-energize all of your life experiences. You will then be able to redefine the crises or challenges that confront you as opportunities for growth, whether they appear at the time as positive or negative experiences.

This perspective is a key to empowerment, allowing you to move beyond the limitation of circumstances. As you reframe your innate power to claim spiritual knowing you begin to move toward a more empowered consciousness. All circumstances may be reframed as containing the potency of self-realization through self-mastery and self-discovery.

From this perspective, you also increase your power of choice. You decide for yourself by the art of framing and reframing your experiences and your definition of yourself as a spiritual rather than limited being. Beyond self-definition is the larger question of how you perceive life and your own journey in spirit through that life. As you gain greater mastery in framing and reframing your experiences, you move your understanding and your mastery to a higher level from which you can see yourself as a spiritual being on a human journey.

You possess the power of choice. If you cannot choose your circumstances, you can choose your attitudes toward those experiences. The power of that choice can be liberating, allowing you to re-conceptualize your journey and the power of Spirit moving through you in your journey.

You may doubt your ability to create, yet ever are you a creator. You become empowered by the act of framing and reframing your consciousness until you clearly see that life does not simply happen to you, but rather you co-create your life with the Divine.

Thus, you are the creator and tender of the force fields of light, and the dormant seeds of power and transformation exist at your core, waiting for an expansion into the light of day. It is only your skepticism about the power of your radiant self that energizes the weed thoughts of negation and chokes the tenuous roots of your flower with deservedness issues. Your worthiness and deservedness are inherent in your nature. The sunlight of your expansive blossoming has begun! The force fields of light —now better tended—will take you to the light of new possibilities. The weed thoughts of unworthiness will shrivel and wither before your greater gaze. The fields of light dance in the possibilities of the day and the possibilities of an empowered you.

www.ingramcontent.com/pod-product-compliance
Lightning Source LLC
LaVergne TN
LVHW021559070426
835507LV00014B/1868